Reader's comments on
"The *Amazing* 2000-Hour Flashlight"
(the 2013 version of this book)

"Perfect." – Virginia Candela

"*I loved it.*" – michael williams

"**Highly** Recommended" – Bernie Carr (the Apartment Prepper blog)

"*Really loved this book.*" – Mark Emerson

"**Highly** recommend" – Avrum and Denise's Farm

"*I loved this!*" – Leslee Stauffer

"**highly** recommend" – stephen j. ladouceur

"*I love it!*" – PD Mitchell

"**HIGHLY** recommend this" – G. Snyder

"*Can't ask for better.*" – LucMee

Other lighting books by Ron Brown –

- **Book 1: Candles** (*The Non-Electric Lighting Series*) available on Amazon as both Kindle and paperback

- **Book 2: Olive Oil Lamps &c.** (*The Non-Electric Lighting Series*) available on Amazon as both Kindle and paperback

- **Book 3: Lamp Fuels** (*The Non-Electric Lighting Series*) available on Amazon as both Kindle and paperback

Note: It's intended that, ultimately, there will be about ten books in *The Non-Electric Lighting Series.*

- **Lanterns, Lamps & Candles: A User's Guide** [available on CD from R&C Publishing]

- **Propane for Preppers** [free; available on Gaye Levy's blog *Backdoor Survival*]
  Part 1 www.backdoorsurvival.com/propane-for-preppers-part-one/
  Part 2 www.backdoorsurvival.com/propane-for-preppers-part-two/
  Part 3 www.backdoorsurvival.com/propane-for-preppers-part-three/
  Part 4 www.backdoorsurvival.com/propane-for-preppers-part-four/
  Part 5 www.backdoorsurvival.com/propane-for-preppers-part-five/

- **Converting a gas lantern to kerosene** [free; YouTube video]

The *NEW* 2000-Hour Flashlight

Ron Brown

R&C Publishing

Newark Valley, New York

Notice: This manual is designed to provide information on flashlights.

It is not the purpose of this guide to reprint all the information that is otherwise available, but to complement, amplify, and supplement other texts and resources. You are urged to read all the available material and learn as much as you can about flashlights and to tailor the information to your specific circumstances.

Every effort has been made to make this guide as complete and accurate as possible. However, there may be mistakes, both typographical and in content. Therefore this text should be used only as a general guide and not as the ultimate source of flashlight modification. Furthermore, this guide contains information that is current only up to the printing date.

The purpose of this manual is to educate and entertain. The views, opinions, positions, and strategies expressed by the author are his alone. The author makes no representations as to the accuracy, completeness, correctness, suitability, or validity of any information in this book and will not be liable for any errors, omissions, or delays in this information or any losses, injuries, or damages arising from its use.

ISBN 978-0-9905564-2-8

Published by
R&C Publishing
15 Dr. Knapp Road South
Newark Valley, NY 13811

Printed in the United States of America

The *NEW* 2000-Hour Flashlight

Table of Contents

Let there be light . . . (Genesis 1:3)

Foreword to the new edition

My interest in Prepping, or what I like to call modern survivalism, began when I moved to an island about 26 miles from the mainland of the United States. It did not take me long to realize that our little island paradise was dependent upon mainland suppliers for everything from food to fuel to basic electrical power.

In an effort to become self-reliant, I sought alternatives that would allow me to get by just fine, thank you very much, without dependence on others. High on the list was ensuring that I had adequate light. The Pacific Northwest can get pretty dark and gloomy.

Early on, I was lucky enough to hook up via email and the internet with Ron Brown and his book, *Lanterns, Lamps and Candles*. (Which, by the way, is an excellent primer on lighting for the do-it-yourselfer.) Later, when he asked if I was interested in a flashlight that would run 1000 hours on a single battery I said "heck yes".

Light is important for day-to-day activities but, in an emergency and especially following a disaster, light is not just a convenience; it is priceless. Having adequate light can be lifesaving when stumbling around in the chaos following a fire, a hurricane, an earthquake, or during a medical emergency.

And so began a many-months-long journey. As it turned out, Ron put together detailed directions for building not just a 1000-hour flashlight but what morphed into *2000-hour* flashlight!

He showed how to do it using simple materials and a nominal amount of skill. The 2000-hour flashlight could be built for less than $10, a trip to the local hardware store, and about half an hour of your time.

But, in the months following publication a glitch developed. The flashlight model used to build the 2000-hour flashlight was replaced with a newer model. So Ron has prepared this update showing, step-by-step, how to extend the run time of several different flashlights. It is an interesting discussion. It turns out there's more than one flashlight that can be modified to run 2000 hours or more. A flashlight that will run around the clock for three months? Now that's something to make you say, "Wow!"

It seems like there is always a blackout somewhere, whether due to a storm, a transformer failure, or even an errant vehicle knocking out a power pole. And yes, those still exist! If every family had a 2000-hour flashlight tucked away with their preps, life would be a whole lot easier for a whole lot of people.

As with all of his books, Ron's objective is to put the best information available into the most possible hands. I urge you to give this book a read and, more importantly, to actually build one of these extended hour flashlights yourself.

It is not that difficult and it will be time and effort well spent.

Gaye Levy

February 2015

*****

Want to learn more about basic preparedness? Please visit Gaye's website at www.backdoorsurvival.com or her Facebook page at www.facebook.com/thesurvivalwoman.

The *NEW* 2000-Hour Flashlight

1.0 Disclaimer

For the record, several brand names and businesses are mentioned in this manual – Energizer, Walmart, Duracell, etc. – but I receive no compensation in any form from any of them. In this manual I simply tell my story as I might tell an office mate at the water cooler.

2.0 Background

The Amazing 2000-Hour Flashlight was first published in 2013. It described a modification or 'hack' to a specific flashlight, the Eveready 5109LS (marked 5X on the wrapper).

The hack involved adding a resistor to the light's circuitry. Doing so produced a flashlight that ran 2000 nonstop hours on one battery. One of the key objectives was to make the instructions user-friendly. Here's what Amazon readers had to say:

- *This book will allow ANYONE to build a 2000-hour flashlight.* – handyman166
- *I did this to one flashlight and my 9 year old son did it by himself to another* – Fireplug
- *Really stupid easy.* – Easy Traveler

Stupid easy? Gee, I hope this new edition can live up to that same high standard.

Unfortunately, in the months following publication of the original book, Eveready brought out newer models and the 5X shuffled off to flashlight heaven. The whole terrible tale is told in Section 7.0.

So what else is out there? Can anything else deliver 2000 hours? Or be modified to do so? Finding out is the purpose behind this revised edition.

3.0 Conclusions

Let's start with the conclusions. Begin with the ending, as it were.

Seeking the longest-lasting flashlight steers us to 6-volt lanterns, the kind with big, square batteries. A bigger battery means more juice.

■ **ABOVE (L to R):** 6-Volt, D, C, AA, AAA. ■

And the longest-lasting light requires alkaline batteries. A new 6-volt lantern of whatever brand comes home from the store with a free battery strapped to its bottom. But the freebie is also a cheapie. An alkaline replacement will last three times longer.

And our search leads to LED bulbs as opposed to traditional incandescent bulbs.

And it points us to economy lights; to the one-LED models. Rayovac, for example, makes both a one-LED lantern and a 10-LED lantern. Which of the two will be the most 'juice-thrifty'?

With the original Eveready 5X no longer on store shelves, possible alternates are:

[1] Eveready's current flavor of the 5109LS.

[2] Rayovac with one LED.

[3] Dorcy with LED upgrade. As purchased, the Dorcy comes with an incandescent bulb.

Illustrated directions are given in this manual for hacking all three of these lights as well as the original 5X. After all, the flashlight you modify will be the one you can get your hands on. Jumping ahead, the test results are:

- Eveready 5X (the original hack) = 2000 hours of useful light ("useful light" is defined in Appendix I)
- Today's Eveready (Section 8.2) = 1100 hours
- Rayovac (Section 8.1) = 2000 hours
- Dorcy (Section 8.3) = 2200 hours

And please, before you run away screaming, "This is over my head," check out Section 11.0 *The Single-Cell Surprise*. It's an off-the-shelf item; no hack required; just unwrap it and go. It might be exactly what you're looking for.

4.0 Here's the problem . . .

■ **ABOVE.** The original Eveready 5109LS marked 5X had two red wires inside the bulb assembly. It was easy to snip one of the wires in half, pull the insulation off each end, and insert a resistor. How easy? Stupid easy. ■

■ **ABOVE.** But the 5109LS now on the store shelves has metal bands inside, not wires. ■

■ **ABOVE.** And the Rayovac LED-model also has metal bands. ■

■ **ABOVE.** And Dorcy doesn't have wires OR metal bands (exactly). What would you call this? Plus upgrading the Dorcy bulb from incandescent to LED is a hassle. ■

■ **ABOVE.** Rayovac makes an adapter that allows us to substitute four D-cells in a 6-volt lantern. ■

The Rayovac adapter, pictured above, is a possible workaround. The adapter yokes four D-cells (each 1.5 volts) in series, thus producing 6 volts.

My Bright Idea is to mount the resistor on the adapter rather than on the flashlight.

Granted, the sum of four D-cells is less mass or weight than one proper 6-volt battery but, with a resistor installed, we can still milk the most light possible out of our batteries.

To test this option, we need to establish what is the longest-lasting D-cell. And that leads us to the topic of batteries.

5.0 Batteries

The purist might object to the way I use the terms 'battery' and 'cell' in this manual. Technically speaking, a battery consists of multiple cells. I'm aware of the distinction but I've chosen to use the terms as they appear in everyday speech. Picture two kids squabbling on the sofa. Mom intervenes. "Fred! Give him back his flashlight cells." Would anybody really say that?

5.1 D-cell test results

As regards D-cell longevity, I tested Duracell, Energizer, and Rayovac side by side (all alkaline). The Duracell D-cell outlasted the other two by a fair margin.

As regards price, Sam's Club had Duracell alkaline D-cells in a 10-pak for $12.40 including sales tax (and it was not an 'on sale' price). That's $1.24 each. Less than any other store. Less than any other brand.

Duracell is thus the winner, providing the biggest bang for the buck amongst alkaline D-cells.

5.2 A little exposé

Although Duracell won the D-cell contest, when it comes to the big, square 6-volt batteries, different story. Typically, 6-volt batteries contain four F-cells.

A reader's comment on Amazon (in regard to the first edition of this book) tipped me off. He noted that Duracell 6-volt batteries contained not four F-cells but four D-cells. I couldn't believe it! In my mind Duracell was the premier brand, $9 at Lowe's; 50% more than the $6 Rayovac at Walmart. So I performed some surgery to get to the bottom of things.

■ **ABOVE.** The Rayovac contains four F-cells. F-cells are the same diameter as D-cells but are longer. ■

■ **ABOVE.** And here's a Duracell with four D-cells inside. Hey! Them cardboard spacers don't come cheap, lemme tell ya. ■

A test showed that, whereas the Rayovac 6-volt gave 2000 hours of useful light (in the original 2000-hour flashlight), a Duracell 6-volt gave only 1100 hours.

Note that the 6-volt Duracell pictured above contains three Duracell Coppertops and one Duracell Procell. From my reading, Coppertops and Procells are interchangeable, built to the same spec. (And it would appear, judging by what I found inside the Duracell 6-volt, that they really are interchangeable. Duracell certainly thinks so.) Why does Duracell market two different brands made to the same spec? Dunno. I guess it's just an example of corporate decision-making in action.

It's also interesting that Duracell advertises a shelf life of ten years for their D-cells. But take those same D-cells and put them in a 6-volt case and, amazingly, the claimed shelf life shrinks to seven years.

But enough scandal mongering. To summarize our test results (in a comparison of Rayovac, Energizer, and Duracell batteries), amongst **alkaline D-cells**, Duracell is both the longest-lasting and carries the lowest price tag. Amongst **alkaline 6-volt batteries**, Rayovac is both the longest-lasting and carries the lowest price tag.

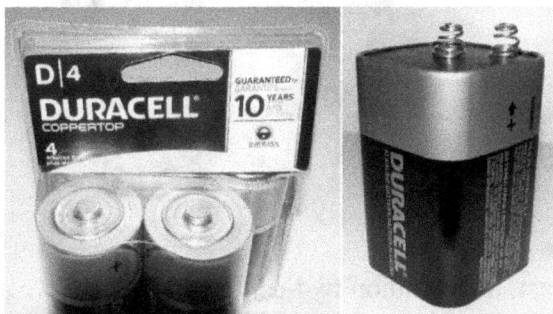

■ **ABOVE LEFT:** Ten-year shelf life. **ABOVE RIGHT:** Seven-year shelf life. ■

6.0 The original hack from 2013

At this point, before considering any newer flashlight models, I want to reproduce (most of) *The Amazing 2000-Hour Flashlight* as it first appeared in 2013. It still contains a lot of useful information.

And who knows? You might just happen across an Eveready 5X – 'new-old stock' – in a hardware store or drug store or farm supply store. In that case, the hack given in Section 6.8 applies word for word.

So here we go.

6.1 The 2000-hour flashlight. What is it?

The original 2000-hour flashlight, described in the first edition of this book, used a specific Eveready flashlight model, a big, square 6-volt battery of the alkaline persuasion, and LED bulbs. Those things, plus a 'resistor' added to the light's circuitry, produced useful light for 2000 non-stop hours.

In contrast, the common two-cell flashlight that we all grew up with in the kitchen drawer, with an incandescent bulb (not LED) and two Heavy Duty D-cells (not alkaline), produced useful light for eight hours. Accidentally leaving it on overnight resulted in dead batteries come morning.

Eight hours is thus the benchmark for flashlight performance most of us have tucked away in our brains. That's why 2000 hours is slightly jaw-dropping.

And what is 'useful light'? The formal standard is defined in Appendix I. For the moment, please know that 'useful light' is sufficient to cook supper, change a car tire, or milk the cows.

6.2 Where can I get one?

You can't buy it. The objective of this book [i.e. both the first edition as well as the current book] is to show you how to build one. It's a hack or modification to an existing light, not a flashlight built from scratch. Another objective is simplicity. It needs to be easy, practical. And the overriding goal is to create the longest-lasting light, not the brightest light.

6.3 How does it work?

It's the resistor that does the doing. The resistor (that we add to the light's circuitry) 'resists' current draw and extends battery life. Of course, reducing current draw reduces light output. So there's a practical limit on how big a resistor can be used. That circles us back around, once again, to our standard; to our definition of 'useful.'

6.4 Who needs it?

For sure a 2000-hour flashlight would be a blessing for people in high-rise apartments.

When I wrote the book *Lanterns, Lamps & Candles: A User's Guide*, I never came fully to grips with the issue of coping with a power outage when living in a high-rise – toting fuel up mega flights of stairs when the elevators weren't working or storing fuel beforehand in a cramped apartment.

A 60-year-old friend of mine lives on the 12th floor of a high-rise. The picture below was taken from her balcony. A lot of people live in high-rises.

Consider, too, underground fallout shelters, the polar opposite of high-rises. People are known to go slightly bonkers if there's no light in a shelter. But ordinary flashlights soon run down and shelter residents must choose between oxygen to breathe and oxygen to burn a candle.

The 2000-hour flashlight doesn't use any oxygen. How long will you stay in your shelter? Two weeks? This flashlight runs 12 weeks.

For sheer economy of operation, there's been nothing cheaper (till now) than a miniature kerosene 'boudoir lamp' (with a round $1/8$" diameter wick). Homemade knock-offs are used around the world because one-third cup of kerosene produces a candle-sized flame for 15 hours. At U.S. prices, that's roughly half a cent per hour.

But the boudoir lamp has been trumped. The operating cost or run rate of the 2000-hour flashlight is 40% less than a kerosene boudoir lamp.

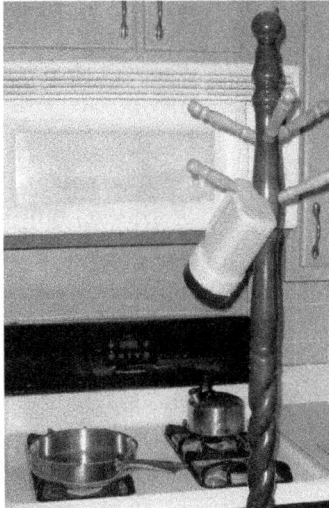

Safety considerations also favor the flashlight. All fire hazards are removed – in the barn with chaff and hay, around children and invalids where it might get knocked over, when fate has been unkind and you find yourself living in your car, or when checking out a potential gas leak after a natural disaster. Not to mention it smells a lot better than kerosene.

6.5 Giving credit where credit is due

For me, the notion of adding a resistor to a flashlight circuit came from a fellow named Luxstar. He has several how-to videos called instructables ('ibles' for short), one of which shows how to make a 360-hour flashlight by soldering a resistor into a flashlight's circuitry:

[http://www.instructables.com/member/luxstar/]

Realistically, I'm sure the idea of adding a resistor to a flashlight circuit didn't originate with Luxstar any more than it did with me.

Flashlight enthusiasts (flashaholics) use all manner of esoteric stuff to convert ordinary flashlights into high-performance flashlights – HID bulbs (high intensity discharge), LiFePO4 batteries, etc. If you Google 'hacking flashlights' you will unseal the magic portal to a whole new universe.

Luxstar soldered a 56-ohm resistor into an Eveready Model 5109LS flashlight (5X flavor) but he didn't upgrade the battery. He used the Super Heavy Duty battery that came with the light. So two thoughts jump to mind. What if we use a bigger resistor, say 150 ohms? And an alkaline battery? As it turns out, those two tweaks are all that is necessary to produce a 2000-hour flashlight.

The icing on the cake is the simplicity of the flashlight's design (i.e. the Eveready 5109LS 5X) plus the simplicity of the modification. Easy to do. Easy to understand.

Even better, unlike the flashaholics, we don't need to solder. We can use wire-glue instead, a black glue that contains carbon and conducts electricity. Wire-glue reduces this undertaking from a techie project to Junior High School level.

Unfortunately, Luxstar doesn't provide much criterion by which to judge the light's performance. He says:

> *"The test started on the morning of 10-26-12. I was expecting a 200 hour run time. After 15 days (360 hours). The flashlight still puts out a usable amount of light. I can still read with it without any problem. I also got the opinion of a fellow flashlight enthusiast who thinks the flashlight is still useful for its intended purpose which is for the user to be able to easily see their way around the house in the dark and be able to easily read. The flashlight is noticeably dimmer than it was at the beginning of the test so I would conclude that this is a 360 hour flashlight."* [sic]

That's a rather ambiguous standard by which to compare other designs. When he says, "the flashlight is noticeably dimmer," for example, he's relying on his memory of how bright it used to be, two weeks earlier.

As mentioned earlier, we'll define the performance standard in Appendix I. Right now, let's end the jawboning and just build one.

6.6 Bill of materials

● **Below.** An Eveready LED flashlight, Model 5109LS [the 5X flavor].

● **Below.** A 150-ohm resistor. The Radio Shack Model No. and Catalog No. are the same: 2711109. Radio Shack's price for a packet of five is $1.49.

● **Below.** Local hobbyist and electronics stores (Radio Shack competitors) also carry resistors. NTE is one brand (from NTE Electronics, Inc., 44 Farrand Street, Bloomfield, NJ 07003). A local hobby store in my area charges $1.25 for a package of six NTE resistors.

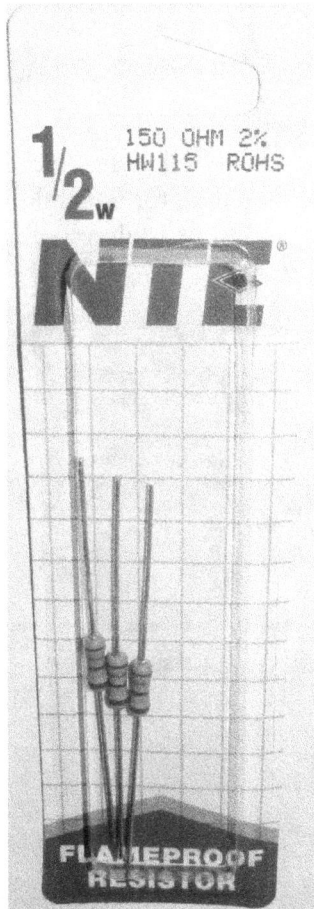

Resistor color-coding is explained in Appendix II.

● **Below.** Conductive wire-glue. The Radio Shack part number is 6400146. Radio Shack's price is $5.49 for 0.3 fluid oz.

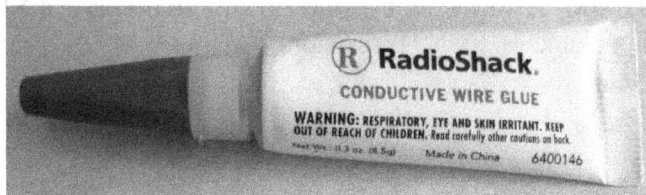

● **Below.** You can also find wire-glue on eBay. It costs about $10, postage included, for 0.3 fluid oz. Below is item # 0400 from Anders Div. of Idolon Tech., 72 Stone Place, Melrose, MA 02176.

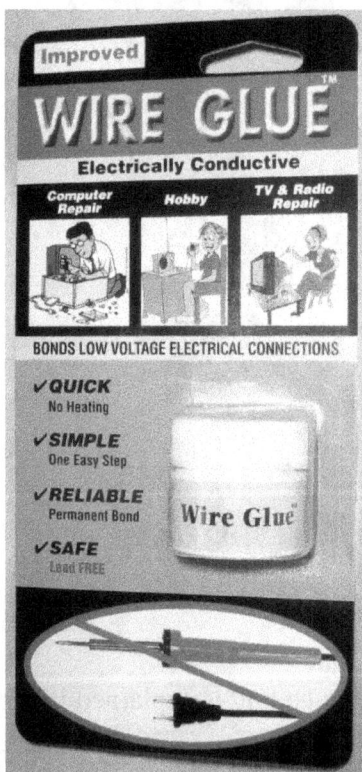

6.7 Tools

- needle-nose pliers
- small sidecutters (pliers) or nail clips
- $^1/_{16}$" drill bit or small nail

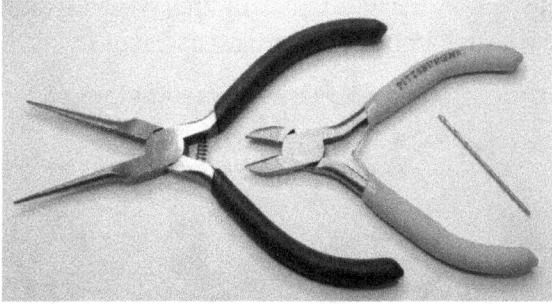

6.8 The hack: how to do it

Step 1

- **Below.** Unscrew the front of the flashlight as if changing the battery. See below. The yellow body (the part that holds the battery), the black collar, and the clear plastic lens can be laid to one side. The assembly that holds the bulb is what we'll work on.

Step 2

• **Below.** We see two red wires on the bulb assembly. We need to cut one of those wires in half so we can insert our resistor into the circuit. If wire cutters are lacking, nail clips can be used for the cutting. Cut the wire in the middle, leaving an equal amount of wire on each side.

Step 3

- **Below.** Next we need to strip the red insulation off the wire ends. We gently but firmly pull on the red insulation. It slides off end-ways. See below.

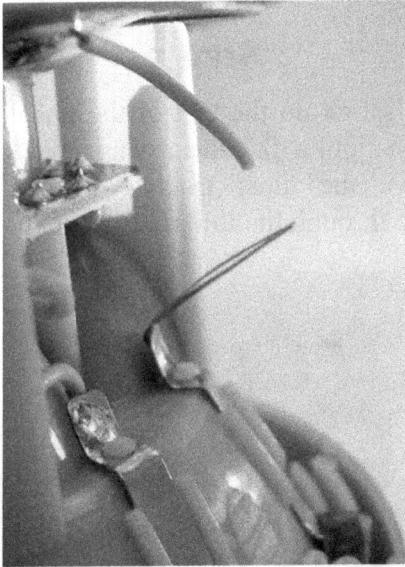

Step 4

- **Below**. Wrap a resistor wire around the shank of a $1/16$" drill bit. It will make about three wraps. Repeat the process with the other resistor leg.

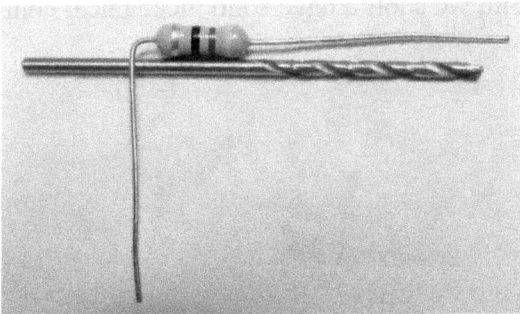

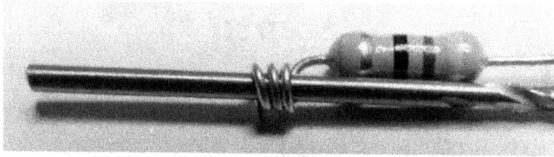

Step 5

• **Below.** Let's first do the end of the flashlight wire that attaches to the light's flat metal ring; that's the end that seems to give the most trouble. Thread the braided flashlight wire through the throat of the "coil spring" in the resistor wire.

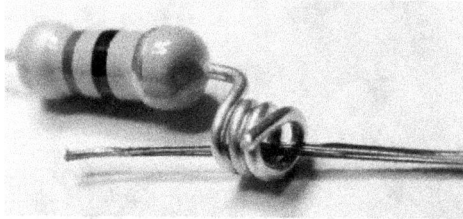

Step 6

• **Below.** With pliers, crush flat the coil spring, trapping the braided flashlight wire inside. Then repeat Step #5 for the other end of the flashlight wire and flatten that end as well. At this point we should have solid mechanical connections.

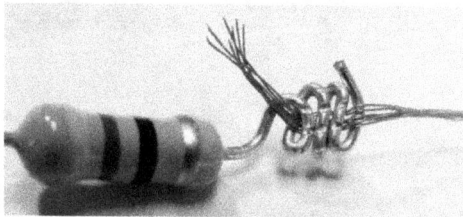

Step 7

● **Below.** Apply a drop of black wire-glue to the joints just formed. The glue is runny stuff so insert a one-inch-wide strip of paper under the wires to shield other components. Be thrifty with the glue. More is not better.

Step 8

● **Below.** After 15 or 20 minutes of drying, the glue will start to harden and you can remove the paper. At this point you can also snip off straggly wire ends. See below. Wow! Wadda connection. Sure is purty, ain't it?

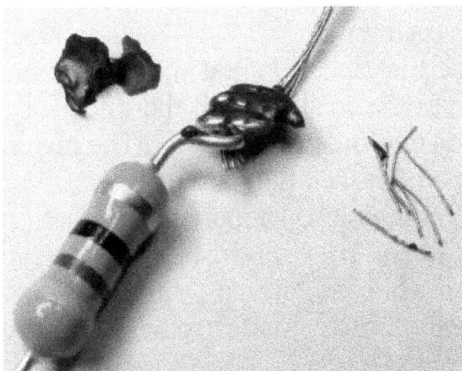

If you leave the paper in the bulb assembly overnight (instead of removing it when the glue becomes tacky) it may become firmly glued in place and need to be cut away with cuticle scissors or a razor blade.

Step 9

The glue needs to dry overnight at room temperature. After that, we can insert a battery into the body of the flashlight, add the newly modified bulb assembly, and screw on the collar/lens assembly (i.e. bezel assembly). We can bend the resistor wires if necessary for clearance but everything the wires touch will be plastic so they don't need to be wrapped or otherwise shielded. *Voila!* A 2000-hour flashlight!

6.9 Clarification

Judging from reader feedback, most people find the instructions in Steps 1-9, above, sufficient. But not everyone. Some say "the directions lack clarity . . . where you add a resistor to your flashlight."

'If you confuse, you lose' (or so the saying goes amongst writers). And if one person is confused, then for sure others are as well. In an effort to make this flashlight modification as clear as possible I've added two photographs (below).

In the first photo, I show a stripped wire (reference Step 3, above) threaded through the throat of the 'spring' we created on one end of the resistor. The picture shows the spring crimped (crushed flat) with pliers.

The crimping is important so that wire-end #1 doesn't decide of its own free will to escape from its spring-prison while you are busy fashioning a second joint with wire-end #2. These wires sometimes have a mind of their own.

The second photo shows the second wire threaded through the throat of the second spring. As shown, the spring has not yet been crimped shut. That would come next.

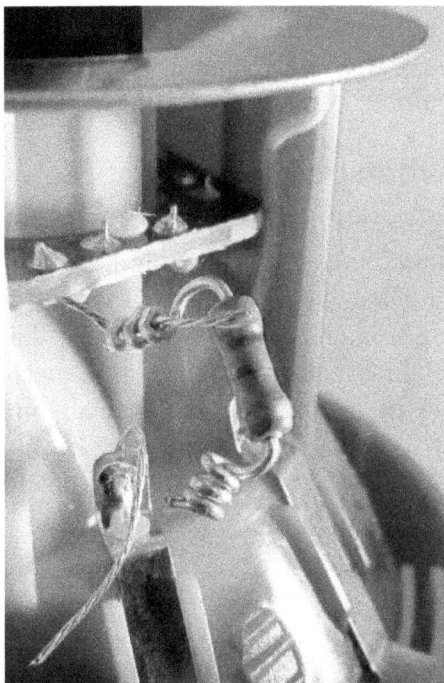
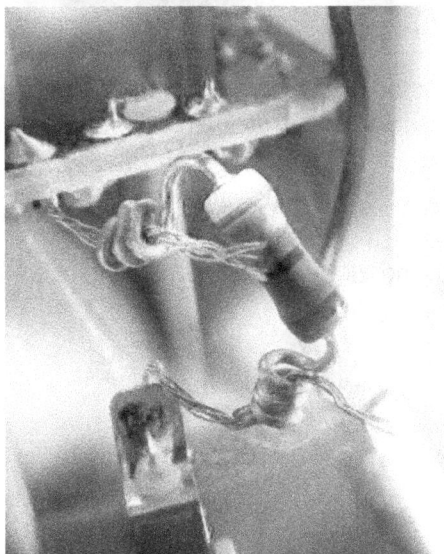

After crimping, wire-glue would be applied to both joints (springs) and the straggly braided wire ends would be trimmed or snipped off.

6.10 For when you get in trouble

One reader broke off the braided wire attached to the metal ring. His solution was to drill a hole in the ring and use a screw to secure that end of the resistor wire. It worked well.

If we use his method, we need to drill a hole. To do that, we must first make a dimple in the metal ring where the hole is to be. Below we see a small block of wood clamped in a vise, backing up the metal ring. A paneling nail has been used as a center punch to dimple the ring.

Drilling comes next. Use a $^5/_{64}$" drill bit. I strongly urge you to employ a hand drill if at all possible (the old eggbeater kind). With an electric drill, the bit, at the precise instant it breaks through the metal, can snag on the metal being drilled and yank the flashlight assembly out of your hands, twirling it around at a frightening rate of speed.

Don't let it happen. Go slow. Wear gloves. Wear goggles. Think safety.

The screws are tiny, $1/4$" long. See below.

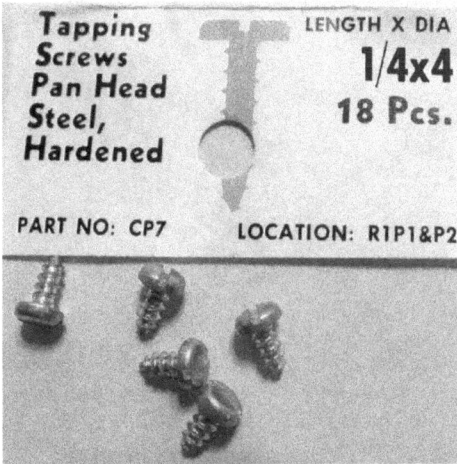

| Tapping Screws Pan Head Steel, Hardened | LENGTH X DIA 1/4x4 18 Pcs. |
| PART NO: CP7 | LOCATION: R1P1&P2 |

Shown below is a resistor wire trapped beneath our screw. The screw can be located anywhere on the ring as long as the end of the other braided flashlight wire is within reach. The screw head does not interfere with the battery terminal which is merely a spring resting on the flat ring.

6.11 Bright mode vs. energy-saver mode

If bright light is preferred over long battery life, here's an easy way to bypass the resistor.

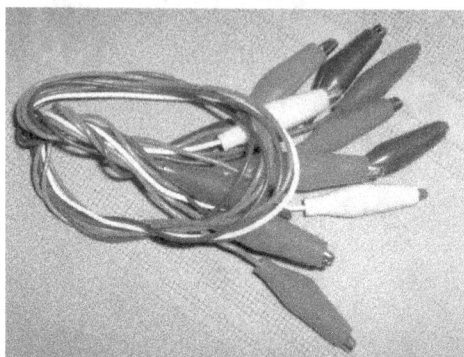

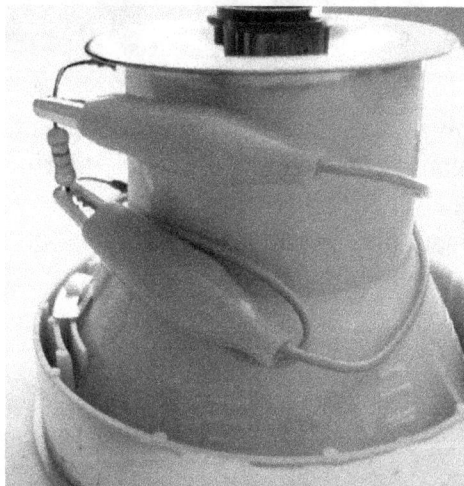

Just one test lead is required, the kind with an alligator clip on each end. Attach alligator #1 to the north side of the resistor. Attach alligator #2 to the south side of the resistor. This provides an alternate path for electricity to flow from the battery to the bulb. Electricity takes the easiest path. The light will shine as if the resistor did not exist.

Wrap the test lead loosely around the bulb assembly. Tuck any surplus lead wire under the lead itself. Then reassemble the light with the test lead inside. *Voila!* Bright mode.

And if we remove the test lead? *Voila!* Energy-saver mode.

7.0 Why a new edition?

The Amazing 2000-Hour Flashlight (2013) was based on the Eveready 5109LS 5X. But the 5X is gone. Let me describe what happened. (You can skip this section if you like. It's basically a history lesson.)

■ **ABOVE.** Eveready has done some fairly dreadful stuff with part numbering. The original hack was based on Eveready Model 5109LS (labeled 5X and claiming 65 hours of run time). The 5X had three LED's. ■

■ **ABOVE.** A second flashlight appeared in mid-2013 (just about the time "The Amazing 2000-Hour Flashlight" was going to press). The new light was also Model 5109LS but was now labeled 10X and claiming 130 hours of run time. It was the same price as the 5X and sold side-by-side with the 5X. And the 10X had three LED's. Both inside and out, the 5X and 10X appeared to be identical; only the labels were different. ■

The 5X has 3 LED's and the 10X has 3 LED's and the newest flavor has one LED. All three have the same Model number (5109LS) and the same UPC barcode. Eveready does have an in-house number (called UPN) to distinguish between them. The 5X UPN is 129718. The 10X UPN is 133485. The one-LED version is UPN 135568. The UPN appears on the label in small print. (And that's the only place it appears. If you remove the peel-off label, neither the 5109LS Model number nor the UPN appear anywhere on the light itself.)

■ **ABOVE.** In late 2014, an Eveready 5109LS with **one** LED appeared. Again, it was sold side-by-side with previous models (5X and 10X). Amazingly, all three of these lights used the same UPC (Universal Product Code) in the barcode. If I recollect correctly (to borrow one of Grandpa's favorite expressions), UPC was intended as a unique product identifier to avoid mix-ups and ambiguity. ■

I'm not the only one confused. When I became aware that 5X's and 10X's were being phased out, I ordered some flashlights from Amazon (i.e. not from a vendor selling on Amazon; from Amazon itself). The online verbal description said 10X although the image displayed a 5X. What arrived in my mailbox were neither 5X's nor 10X's. They were the new one-LED models. Hey! UPC is UPC is UPC, no?

Shortly after that, a (more or less) local Home Depot said (on-line) they had 5X's in stock. I would find (so they said) over a hundred of them in aisle RC, bay 001.

Home Depot's computerized inventory system was misinformed. Oops. Turned out they had not 5X's in stock but the new one-LED version. All over the store. In aisle

RC, bay 001. On end caps. Near the cash registers. Razzlefrats! I drove 30 miles to get there.

■ **ABOVE LEFT:** The newest 5109LS (one LED) contains flat metal bands rather than red wires. And the competing brands (Rayovac, Dorcy) also have flat metal bands. When I originally wrote "The Amazing 2000-Hour Flashlight" I did not readily see how the metal bands could be cut-and-spliced so I ignored all of the flat-metal-band lights. But now I have no choice. Flat metal bands (of various styles and designs and brands) are the only things that remain. **ABOVE RIGHT:** Turns out that flat-metal-band lights can indeed be hacked. But will anything on the market today approach 2000 hours? ■

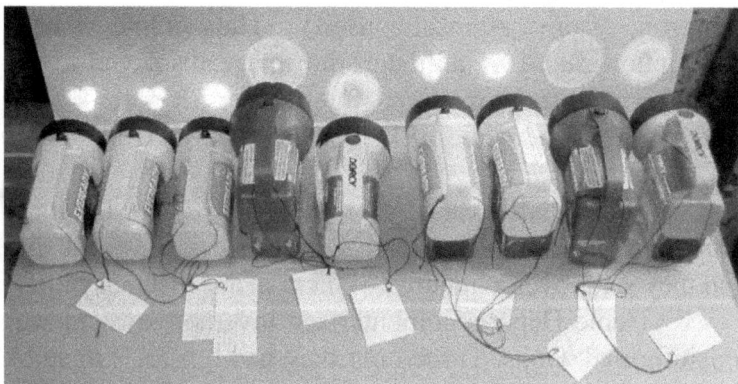

■ **ABOVE.** Looks like we have some testing to do. ■

8.0 The new hacks

8.1 Rayovac

So let's get down to cases. We'll start with the easiest hack – Rayovac.

8.1.1 Bill of materials for Rayovac

• **Resistor.** The resistor will be a 150-ohm resistor, the same as was used in the original 2000-hour flashlight. See Section 6.6.

• **Wire glue or solder.** Wire glue is described in Section 6.6. The alternative is solder, discussed in Appendix III.

• **Flashlight.** The flashlight is a Rayovac Model EFL6V-BLW. Caution. Rayovac makes three different 6-volt lanterns that look similar. The one we want is Model EFL6V-BLW (shown below). We **do not** want Model EFL6V-BA with an *incandescent* bulb. And we **do not** want Model EFL6V10LED-B with *ten* LED's.

8.1.2 Tools for Rayovac

- Wire cutters (pictured in Section 6.7).
- Tin snips or (better yet) 'Chinese scissors' as described/pictured in Appendix III.
- Soldering iron (described/pictured in Appendix III). Necessary if we use solder instead of wire glue.

8.1.3 The Rayovac hack: how to do it

Step 1

- **Below.** Cut one of the flat metal bands. (I'm demonstrating this using 'Chinese scissors' because the mere tip of the scissors will do the job. That means very little clearance is required.)

● **Below.** We're still on Step #1 here. The Chinese scissors give a crisp, clean cut.

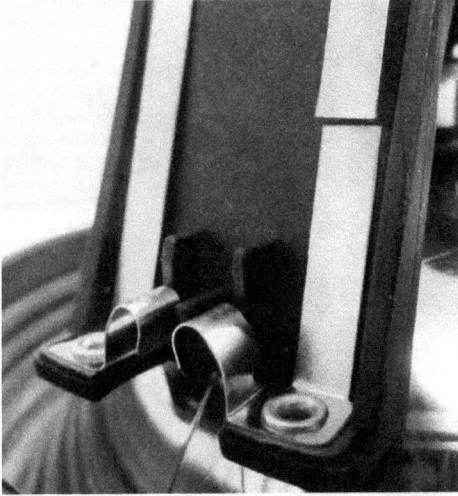

Step 2

● **Below.** Curl each of the cut ends into a loop. Here I used needlenose pliers.

Step 3

● **Below.** Bend the resistor legs as needed and insert them into the loops.

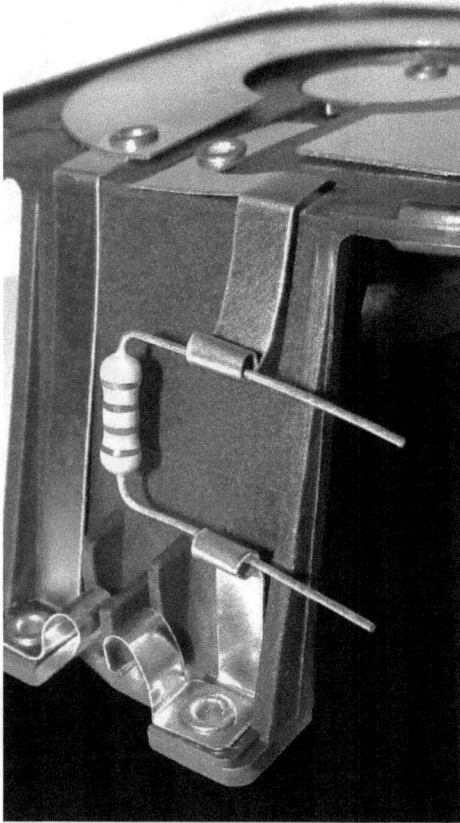

Step 4

● **Below.** Crush the loops flat with pliers. Solder the resistor legs in place or use wire glue. Snip off the ends of the resistor legs with wire cutters. You're done. Put a battery in your lantern and light up the night.

8.1.4 Rayovac results

The Rayovac EFL6V-BLW with a 150-ohm resistor produces useful light for 2000 hours, equal to the original 2000-hour flashlight. Please note, this result is obtained with a Rayovac 6-volt alkaline battery; not the factory-issue "Rayovac General Purpose" battery that comes strapped to the bottom of the light.

The Rayovac hack is simpler and faster and requires less tools than the Dorcy hack. The Rayovac lantern design, with its metal rivets, is robust; it will take some 'abuse' in the hacking process. And the Rayovac flashlight is more widely sold or distributed, easier to find, than Dorcy.

Should you, in a SHTF scenario, convert a dozen lights for a dozen family members, these features (flashlight availability, ease of conversion) favor the Rayovac.

8.2 Eveready 5109LS with 1 LED

The Eveready modification is virtually identical to the Rayovac modification just described.

● The **How-To fabrication steps** are the same: (1) cut one of the flat metal bands, (2) curl each cut end into a loop, (3) insert the two legs of a 150-ohm resistor into the two loops, (4) crush the loops flat with pliers, and (5) secure the loop-joints with solder or wire-glue.

● The **Tools** are the same: wire cutters; tin snips; soldering iron.

● The **Bill of Materials** is the same: 150-ohm resistor; wire glue or solder; flashlight. *Aha!* There's a difference! The flashlight! In this case we'll be using an Eveready 5109LS with one LED.

■ **ABOVE.** The light under consideration here is the Eveready 5109LS, UPN 135568, with one LED. ■

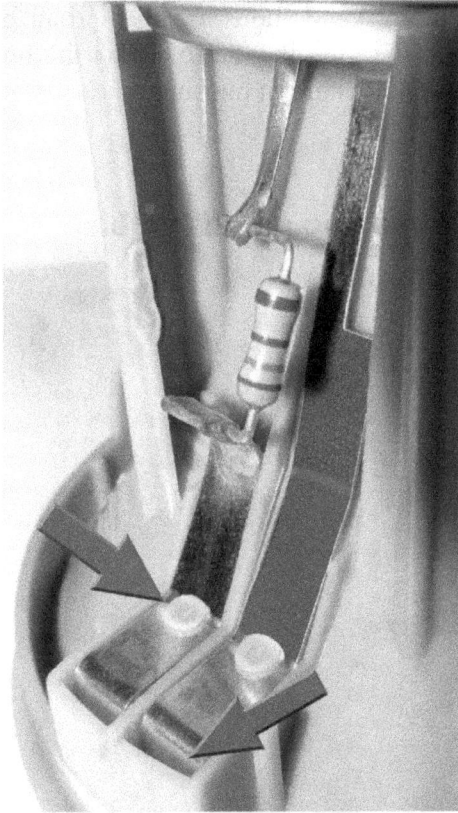

■ **ABOVE.** Here's the hack at the end. The flat metal band was cut, the ends curled, a resistor inserted and soldered in place. No problem. (The smudge on the plastic to the left of the resistor is where I accidentally touched the hot soldering iron to the plastic frame.) ■

But trouble lurks. Where the Rayovac had metal rivets the Eveready has plastic. That's what the left-hand arrow points to – a plastic rivet-head. Where the Rayovac could survive rough handling, the Eveready breaks.

If the plastic rivet-head snaps off (and it happens; trust me), the metal band essentially falls out of the lantern. Then what? My fix is to fill the little well (that's what the right-hand arrow points to) with hot-melt glue or epoxy. Glue the metal band back in place. That section of metal band is important. The short stretch of road between the rivet-head and the glue is what contacts the on-off switch mounted back in the lantern housing.

8.2.1 For when you get in trouble

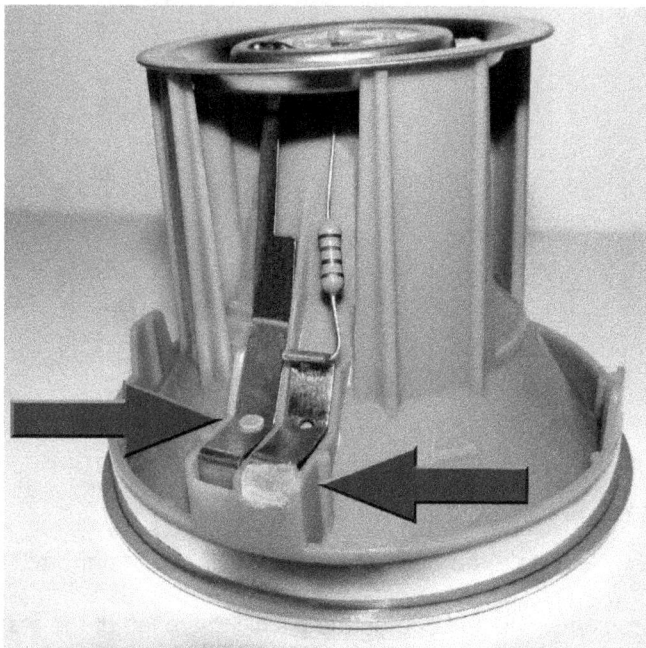

■ **ABOVE.** Here's a hack where everything that could go wrong did go wrong. Shown here is the end of the job after it was all fixed. The left arrow points to the good rivet-head; the one that wasn't disturbed and is still in place. On the right-hand band the rivet-head is gone; only a hole remains. The right arrow points to the little well, now filled with hot-melt glue that holds the band in place. Note the top half of the metal band is gone entirely. It simply came loose and fell out. ■

■ **ABOVE.** I replaced the half-band that fell out with a resistor leg. I drilled down through the 'roof' of the assembly with a #60 drill bit (discussed in Appendix III), inserted a resistor leg (pushing it up through the ceiling from underneath), bent a small 'foot' in the end of the leg, and soldered the foot in place. The arrow on the right points to my soldered foot. On the left is the factory-solder on the metal band that was not disturbed. ■

■ **ABOVE.** If we flip the bulb assembly upside down the arrow points to where the drill bit came through the ceiling. And where the resistor-leg now goes through the hole we made. ■

Okay, so it ain't beautiful. But when you push the switch the light comes on. Drum roll, please.

8.2.2 Eveready results

The 5109LS with one LED (UPN 135586) plus a 150-ohm resistor provides useful light for 1100 hours (just over half what the original 5109LS 5X produced). Please note, this result is obtained with a Rayovac 6-volt alkaline battery; not the factory-issue "Eveready Super Heavy Duty" battery that comes strapped to the bottom of the light.

8.3 Dorcy

Dorcy makes a 6-volt lantern they call the 'Luminator.' Unfortunately, the Luminator comes from the store with an incandescent bulb that must be replaced with an LED. And the way we add a resistor is quite different from any of the other lights discussed so far. So, although the Dorcy turns out to be the longest-lasting flashlight, its hack is the most complicated.

8.3.1 Bill of materials for Dorcy

● **Insulated wire.** We need a strand of insulated wire. A 12-inch length of common extension cord will work but it's only a single strand we need, not a doubled strand.

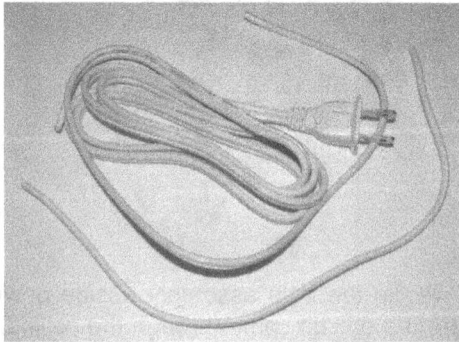

● **Resistor.** The resistor will be a 150-ohm resistor, the same as described in Section 6.6.

● **Tape or heat-shrink tubing** (below). Black electrical tape will work as will a 2-inch length of heat shrink tubing.

● **LED bulb.** As purchased, the Dorcy has an incandescent bulb. It must be replaced with an LED bulb. What I used was a Rayovac 4V6VLED-1T sold by Walmart.

- **Solder.** Discussed in Appendix III.

- **Dorcy lantern –**

■ **ABOVE.** Dorcy Luminator, Model 41-2087. I've seen them at Family Dollar as well as Sears. ■

8.3.2 Tools for Dorcy

- Wire cutters (pictured in Section 6.7).

- Soldering iron (see Appendix III for picture and discussion).

- Knife (below) to cut insulation from wire ends as well as cutting tape or heat-shrink tubing.

• 2 small screwdrivers to help change the bulb from incandescent to LED. The screwdrivers pictured below were actually filed down at an earlier date to use on eyeglass frames.

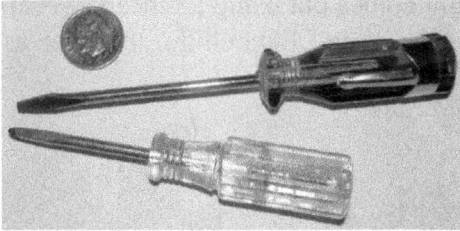

• Heat gun, pictured below. Necessary if heat-shrink tubing is used. A hair dryer will also work (*maybe*).

8.3.3 Changing the Dorcy bulb to LED

One of the things I discovered early on with a Dorcy flashlight was that the 150-ohm resistor doesn't work with the factory-installed incandescent bulb. With the resistor in place, no light comes out using an incandescent bulb. As in zero. You must use an LED bulb for this hack to work.

■ **ABOVE.** The Dorcy Luminator comes with a pointy-nose incandescent bulb (left). It must be replaced with a round-nose LED bulb (right). ■

When you take a Dorcy lantern apart to install a battery, what appears to be a single piece (holding the bulb and the lens) is really a joined set of two distinct assemblies: (1) the 'bezel assembly' holding the lens and (2) the 'bulb assembly' holding the bulb. The two are joined by plastic clips or ears, cast into the bulb assembly.

I found these assemblies difficult to photograph because both of them (as well as the clips) are black in color. I was photographing black on black.

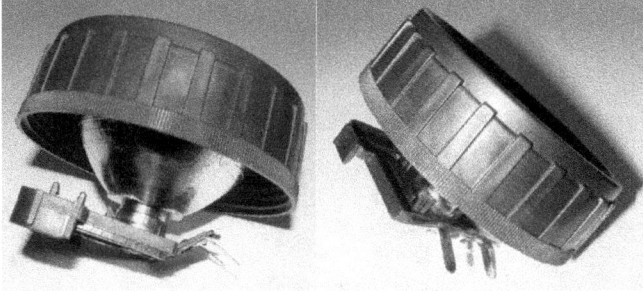

■ **ABOVE.** Here, seen from two different angles, is what appears to be one piece. ■

■ **ABOVE.** But when we get it apart, we discover it's really two pieces – the bulb assembly on the left and the bezel assembly, holding the lens, on the right. ■

In the beginning, I was afraid of breaking off the clips by prying too vigorously. They're only plastic, after all. But it turns out the design is quite robust. By now I've changed the bulb on several 6-volt lights (of similar design) and have yet to break a clip on any of them. Oops! Yes I did. The one I dropped on the concrete floor.

■ **ABOVE.** Here's the bulb assembly alone. The 'clips' are indicated by arrows. There are three clips in total; here we can see two; the third is hidden behind the bulb. To take the two assemblies apart, pry back on these clips until two of the three release the bezel-shoulder onto which they are hooked. It's a tight fit. ■

■ **ABOVE.** This image shows the bezel assembly still hooked to the bulb assembly. The clip on the right (and the shoulder it is holding) is fairly distinct in profile. The clip on the left is a three-quarter view from behind and it is perhaps not so obvious as to what we're looking at. To separate the assemblies, insert small screwdrivers behind two clips (that is, between the clip and the bezel shoulder) and twist or pry on both screwdrivers simultaneously. The camming action will lever open the clips and allow the shoulder to escape. Some strength is required. Bad language is optional. ■

■ **ABOVE.** This shows (at bottom) the shoulder of the bezel assembly from which we are prying loose the bulb assembly. This shoulder is what the clips hook onto. ■

■ **ABOVE.** This is the bulb assembly after being separated from the bezel assembly. The arrow points to a metal keeper-spring that holds the bulb in place. Simply pull on the incandescent bulb to remove it. When we insert the replacement LED bulb, however, we'll need to pry back the keeper. (The bulb shown here is the replacement LED.) ■

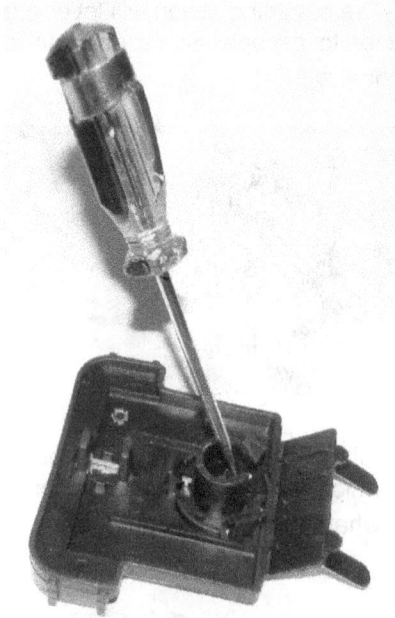

■ **ABOVE.** A screwdriver in bulb-keeper pry-mode. ■

■ **ABOVE.** This is the bezel assembly, ready to receive the bulb assembly (which should now be holding an LED bulb). ■

■ **ABOVE.** Here's the bulb assembly, bottom end up. The bulb itself is underneath, pointing downwards and positioned over the center hole in the bezel assembly. We insert the bulb into the hole, line up the clips with the bezel-assembly shoulders, and give a firm downward push. That spreads the clips and snaps the bulb assembly into place. *Click!* Just like snapping your fingers. Now tell me the truth. Wasn't that easy? ■

8.3.4 Adding the resistor to Dorcy

The Dorcy hack is quite different than what we've done with the other lanterns. With Dorcy, instead of cutting a flat metal band, we're going to run a wire from the switch (inside the lantern body) to one of the tabs on the bulb assembly. It's really not too bad if we use the 'sweat soldering' technique described in Appendix III (q.v.).

After that we'll cut the wire in half and insert the 150-ohm resistor in line. When we're all done and we open the flashlight (to install a battery, say), we're not going to unhook the wire; we're going to leave it in place.

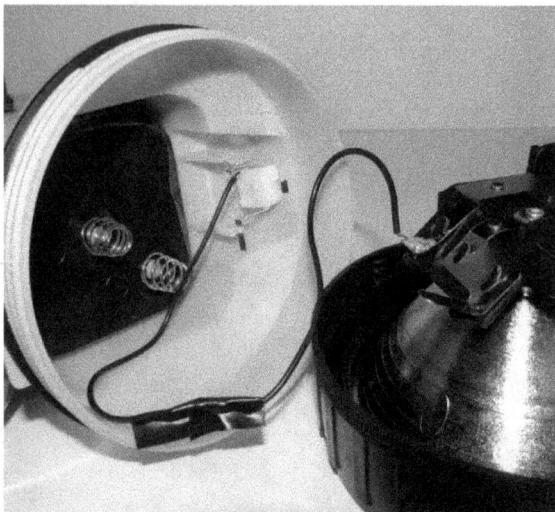

■ **ABOVE.** Here we see a wire running from the switch mounted in the flashlight's housing to a tab on the bulb assembly. When we open the light to change the battery, the wire stays in place. (And when we close the light, we do it very, very carefully.) We also see here the resistor (lower center) covered with black plastic electrical tape. We could use heat-shrink tubing rather than tape.■

■ **ABOVE.** The wire has been cut, the insulation stripped back, and a 150-ohm resistor soldered in place. We can also join the wires to the resistor using the technique employed with the original hack in Section 6.8, above. ■

■ **ABOVE.** As mentioned earlier, the resistor can be covered with heat-shrink tubing (shown here) rather than black plastic electrical tape. The tubing gives a more professional appearance. ■

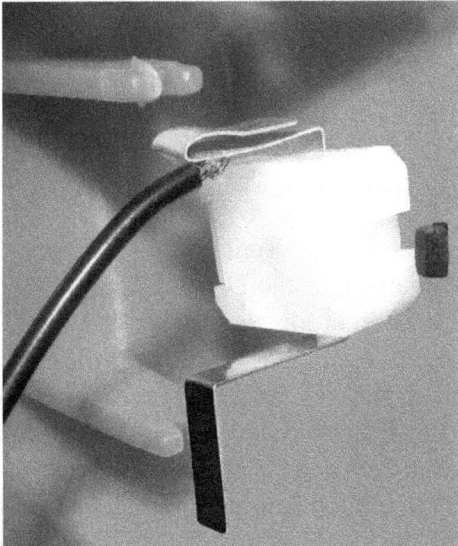

■ **ABOVE.** This shows one end of the wire 'sweat-soldered' to the switch in the housing. Were I to use wire-glue I would insert the wire end into the channel formed by the switch-bracket and pinch it shut with pliers before gluing. Not necessary with 'sweat soldering.' ■

■ **ABOVE.** The other end of the wire is soldered to the tab in the bulb assembly. The tab itself has been folded out of the way. (In fact, some extra tab length was snipped off and discarded.) ■

At this point the job is done. Put in a battery and go deliver a baby. Or husk some corn. Or rosin up the bow for 'Faded Love' and let's all dance.

8.3.5 Dorcy results

The factory-issue Dorcy comes with an incandescent bulb. Upgraded with an LED, the Dorcy Luminator 41-2087 plus a 150-ohm resistor produces useful light for 2200 hours, better than the original 2000-hour flashlight. Please note, this result is obtained with a Rayovac 6-volt alkaline battery; not the factory-issue "Dorcy Heavy Duty" battery that comes strapped to the bottom of the light.

The Dorcy hack is more complicated than the others but produces the best results. More than longevity, the hacked Dorcy is noticeably brighter – at every stage of the game – than the Rayovac or Eveready. After writing this book I have (as you can imagine) a fair collection of flashlights to choose from. And it's a hacked Dorcy that sets beside my kitchen door.

9.0 Hacking the Rayovac adapter

One advantage of hacking a Rayovac adapter is that the adapter can be moved between lanterns. If you hack a lantern, each individual flashlight must be modified. Another advantage is that D-cells are easy to find.

Step 1

■ ABOVE. The line shows where we'll make a saw cut. ■

Step 2

■ **ABOVE.** This is a hack with a hacksaw. Just a blade works fine; you don't need the entire saw. Cut through the plastic up to the metal band and then cut the band. ■

Step 3

■ **ABOVE.** Both halves of the metal band must be curled (with needlenose pliers) into a loop although in this photo only one side has been done. The loops will receive the wire legs of the resistor. ■

Step 4

■ **ABOVE.** Insert the two 'legs' of the resistor into the two loops and crush the loops flat with pliers. After that, trim off the excess leg-length with wire cutters and finish the job with either solder or wire-glue. It's not necessary to mend the saw cut in any way; the adapter is strong enough that it functions perfectly even with a saw cut. ■

9.1 Rayovac adapter results

■ **ABOVE.** Rayovac adapters ready for testing. All with a 150-ohm resistor and four Duracell D-cells. ■

RESULTS:

● The lantern used in the original hack (Eveready 5109LS 5X) gave 1100 hours of useful light using a Rayovac adapter, a 150-ohm resistor, and four Duracell D-cells.

● Today's Eveready 5109LS with one LED gave 600 hours.

● Both (1) the Rayovac one-LED lantern and (2) the Dorcy lantern with LED upgrade performed on par with the Eveready 5109LS 5X (that is, 1100 hours).

10.0 Batteries revisited

10.1 AA & AAA adapters

It sometimes seems like we can run anything from anything given enough battery adapters. An hour on eBay will make you dizzy with the possibilities.

■ **ABOVE:** Here we have AA's adapted to run as D-cells. Then, as D-cells, they can be loaded into a Rayovac 6-volt adapter and used to replace a 6-volt battery. A similar AAA-to-D-cell adapter is also available. Whoda thunk? ■

10.2 Lithium batteries

Flashlight batteries of the zinc-carbon type (General Purpose) and zinc-chloride (Heavy Duty) hark back to the World War II era. They are still made today. Alkaline batteries, introduced in the 1960's, cost more and last longer.

Lithium batteries, introduced in the 1990's, raised the performance bar once again. Some lithium batteries are intended to be rechargeable; others, disposable. They last longer than alkaline but are only available in the smaller sizes (that is, smaller than 'C').

Question is, are lithium AA's part of the conversation when it comes to a long-life flashlight? A small lithium AA carries a higher price tag than does a big alkaline D-cell.

■ **ABOVE.** Lithium AA's are $19.98 for a package of 12 at Sam's Club. With sales tax, that's $1.80 per battery or $7.20 for a set of four. Mounted in AA-to-D-cell adapters and thence in a D-cell-to-6-volt adapter, an Eveready 5109LS 5X (the original 2000-hour flashlight equipped with a 150-ohm resistor) will run 200 hours on four lithium AA's. That's a run rate of 3.6 cents per hour. The same flashlight will run 2000 hours on a $6 Rayovac alkaline 6-volt. That's a run rate of 0.3 cents per hour. So, mechanically, will it work? Yes. Is it cost effective? No. Then again, if you're stranded along the road after dark changing a flat tire, who cares? ■

10.3 C-cell 'adapter'

■ **ABOVE.** The most difficult adapter to find is one allowing C-cells to be substituted for D-cells. As it turns out, U.S. quarters (coins) can often be used as spacers. Seven quarters plus a C-cell comes very close to the length of a D-cell. ■

10.4 9-volt batteries

■ ABOVE. Small, square 9-volt batteries (the kind used in six-transistor radios back in the day) cannot be used in 6-volt hacks because six volts is the requirement, not nine. As a consequence, 9-volt batteries are not part of our discussion. ■

Pak-Lite and Blocklight are two brands of small LED flashlights that do employ the square, 9-volt batteries. And they are certainly handy for pocket or purse. But for sheer longevity, which is the center of our discussion here, the small 1.5-ounce 9-volt batteries can't compete with the 6-volt 2-pounders.

10.5 Refrigerating batteries

Another battery topic worthy of note. Storage. Does it pay to refrigerate or freeze flashlight batteries?

The answer is no, it doesn't pay. It's a waste of time.

I bought six Eveready 'Super Heavy Duty' batteries (D-cells). Two went in the fridge, two in the freezer, two in the cabinet over the kitchen stove. Two years, eight months, and three days later I decided the time was right for testing. I put all six batteries on the dining room table for 48 hours so they could equalize in temperature. I then put the batteries in identical flashlights with incandescent bulbs and tested them side by side. There was little if any difference in results. They all lasted six hours and died. Too bad, so sad. Grandma was wrong.

EXCEPTION. What was just said, directly above, is true for non-rechargeable batteries (zinc-carbon, zinc-chloride, and alkaline) but is not true for rechargeables. At room temperature, NiMH and Nicad batteries begin to lose power within a few days of being charged. But they'll retain 90% for several months if kept in the freezer. Just don't neglect to warm them up to room temperature before using them.

10.6 Rechargeable 6-volt batteries

Rechargeable 6-volt batteries are available. You can use a charger designed for auto batteries (as long as the charger has an option to toggle back and forth between 12-volts and 6-volts).

6-volt batteries are made with several terminal types. To make proper contact inside your lantern you need a battery with spring-type terminals (called 'spring top' by sellers).

■ **ABOVE.** Both of these rechargeable 6-volt lantern batteries are sealed lead-acid (not Nicad and not NiMH). Walmart carries the Rayovac brand for $10. Others are available on eBay. With shipping, they run around $20. Their typical use is in outdoor game feeders of the type made by Moultrie and sold by Cabela's. Both of the batteries shown here weigh in at 1 lb. 11 oz. and both have the same rating (5 amp-hours). ■

■ **ABOVE.** Another way to get the rechargeable feature for your 6-volt lantern is to use rechargeable D-cells in a Rayovac 6-volt adapter. ■

11.0 Single-cell surprise

We're going to break away from our regularly scheduled programing for a moment.

Earlier (in Section 5.0) we tested D-cells to identify which was best to use in the Rayovac 6-volt adapter. I performed the D-cell test using Eveready single-cell flashlights. Although my intent was to compare batteries, it turned out to be the flashlight that surprised me.

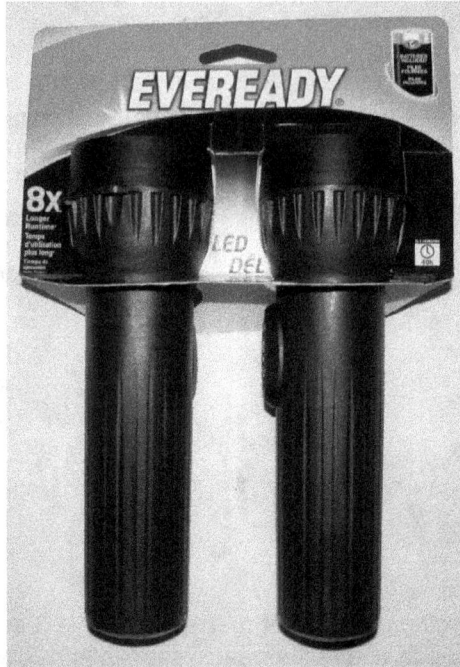

■ **ABOVE.** These flashlights hold only one battery, not two. If you remember from Section 5.1, the winner of the D-cell contest turned out to be Duracell. And one Duracell D-cell in one of these single-cell flashlights gave 160 continuous hours of useable light. That's nearly a week (7 days x 24 hours = 168). ■

These Eveready single-cell LED flashlights are $4.97 (for a two-pak) at Valu Home Center. The run rate for a $1.24 Duracell battery (from Sam's Club) that lasts 160 hours is $8/10$ of a cent per hour. That's cheaper than candles. With zero fire hazard. And it stays lit in the wind.

Rayovac and Dorcy also make single-cell D-cell flashlights but were outperformed by Eveready. The Eveready (above) gave useful light for a week. Rayovac gave useful light for 5 days and Dorcy, 4 days (all using one Duracell battery).

■ **ABOVE.** Rayovac makes a single-cell LED flashlight ($2.97 at Walmart) but it was out-performed by the Eveready.■

■ **ABOVE.** Dorcy also makes a single-cell LED light ($4.65 at Family Dollar). The Dorcy has 3 LED's. As regards run time, it, too, was out-performed by the Eveready. ■

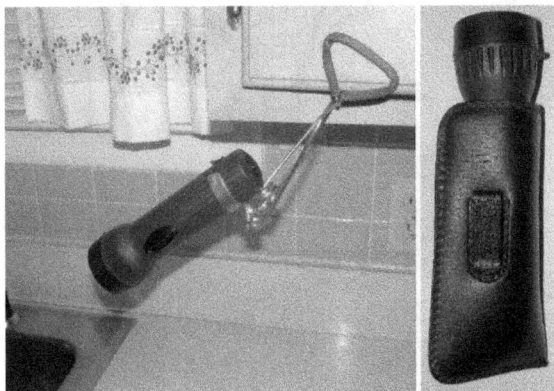

088

■ **ABOVE LEFT:** In a blackout, your 110-volt AC 'clamp light' out in the shop (the one with the aluminum reflector bowl) won't be of much benefit. But you can still make good use of the clamp. **ABOVE RIGHT:** An old eyeglass case makes a fair flashlight holster. A couple of slits cut close to the top (to thread your belt through) works better than the belt loop shown here. ■

Many people need look no further than this for their emergency flashlight. It's cheap. It's an off-the-shelf item. No modification is necessary. One of these flashlights plus a 10-pak of Duracells will provide continuous light, night and day, for over nine weeks. Not too shabby.

One caveat. As we saw in Section 7.0, Eveready has a propensity for tricky numbering. Make sure you get Eveready UPN 132295. That, and only that, is the light under discussion here.

Whilst on the thrifty theme, you might want to save used D-cells for use in this light. When D-cells no longer have enough oomph to power the kids' Christmas toys it's a pretty safe bet that, even then, there's some energy left. UPN 132295 will extract every last drop of remaining juice.

■ **ABOVE.** Castoff D-cells store nicely in an empty plastic coffee can. The 2 lb. 10.5 oz. size will hold 41 batteries (three layers of 14 + 14 + 13) separated by plastic spacers cut from old lids. Full, it weighs over ten pounds. Even with used batteries you're looking at many hours of light. ■

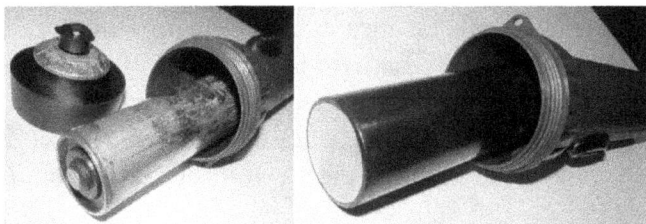

■ **ABOVE.** In a single-cell Eveready flashlight you can even use an F-cell (out of a big 6-volt battery). And you can do the same thing with Dorcy. But not Rayovac; an F-cell does not fit in a single-cell Rayovac. ■

■ **ABOVE.** You may need a spacer (I used a small nut) in the single-cell flashlight to make contact with an F-cell battery terminal. ■

Incidentally, don't modify any of these single-cell flashlights to hold two D-cells. Two D-cells in series would produce 3 volts and the bulbs in these lights are sized for 1.5 volts.

12.0 Using a 12-volt car battery

Here's another pregnant idea. Remember my comment back in the beginning (Section 3.0 *Conclusions*)? "Seeking the longest-lasting flashlight steers us to 6-volt lanterns, the kind with big, square batteries. A bigger battery means more juice."

Let's carry that idea a step further. Why not run a wire from our 6-volt flashlight to a 6-volt golf-cart battery? Farm tractors also use 6-volt lead-acid batteries. These are 40-lb. batteries, not 2-lb. batteries. *Pro rata*, if a 2-lb. battery runs three months, then a 40-lb. battery should run five years.

That pencils out as the cheapest light source known. I'm not saying this could change the world or anything but, ya know, this could change the world.

And car batteries (12 volts) are more common than golf-cart batteries (6 volts). Can we use a step-down transformer to convert 12 volts to six? Yes. And why must the LED bulb be located inside a flashlight? Well, to tell you the truth, it needn't be. With minimal tinkering, we can get a 6-volt LED bulb to run directly off a 12-volt car battery, no flashlight housing required.

This section will show you how. You can have a separate bulb in every room, all running off the same battery. The bulbs can be switched on and off independently and the battery can be located outside or at a distance.

CAUTION. If Junior-High science terms like ohm's law, direct current, and polarity throw you off stride then you might want to skip this particular hack.

But let's get started. We'll work from the battery to the bulb.

■ **ABOVE.** This is a 12-volt deep-cell marine battery. The clip with the red handles is clamped on the positive terminal. Repeat after me: RED ALWAYS GOES TO POSITIVE. ■

■ **ABOVE.** On the left side we see a 'battery clip-on power socket.' You'll need to remember that term if you ever search eBay for this item. On the right is a transformer that will convert 12-volt auto current into 6-volt flashlight current. The transformer is designed to plug into a car's cigarette lighter. But for our purposes we'll plug it into the 'power socket' and clip the power socket to the battery terminals. ■

■ **ABOVE.** This is our 'step-down DC/DC 12-volt/6-volt' transformer, Philmore brand, Model No. BE164, $10.50 at an electronics hobby store. It comes with an assortment of plugs (shown on the left) and a universal plug (for lack of a better term) on the end of the wire (lower right). We're going to snip off the universal plug and splice the transformer-wire to a female socket 'stolen' from a common extension cord. ■

Ordinary extension cords are called 'zip cords' because they consist of two separate wires, each of which is insulated. The two strands are linked by a thin bridge of insulation. If you slice through the bridge and pull, you can separate the two strands – almost like unzipping a zipper. Hence the name.

If you examine the two strands, you'll find that one is smooth and the other has tiny grooves or ridges ('ribbing') running lengthwise of the wire. In DC electricity (which is what flashlights are), convention has it that the ribbed strand is negative. The smooth strand is positive.

That's for the extension cord. If you separate the two zip-strands coming from the transformer, you'll find that one wire is striped (black-and-white in this case) and the other strand is solid black. Convention has it that, in DC electricity, the solid-color strand is negative. The striped wire is positive.

To keep our polarity straight, the black-and white striped wire from the transformer will be married to the smooth wire from the extension cord. This is the positive side.

The solid-color wire (black in this case) from the transformer will be wed to the ribbed strand from the extension cord. This is the negative side and must ultimately be matched to the center terminal of the LED bulb.

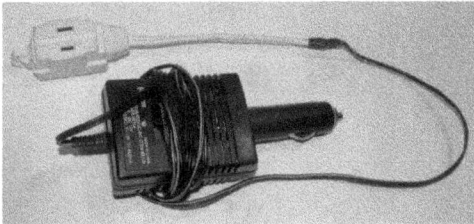

■ ABOVE. Here we have the cut-off end of the transformer wire spliced onto the cut-off female-socket from an extension cord. ■

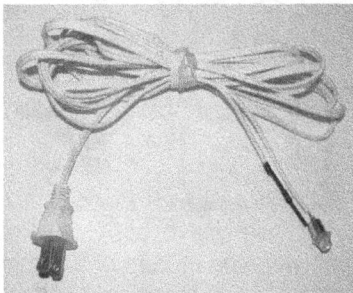

■ ABOVE. We cut off the female socket from the end of an extension cord (and used it on the transformer). But we're not going to throw the cord away. We'll now mount our LED bulb and resistor on the cut end of that cord. ■

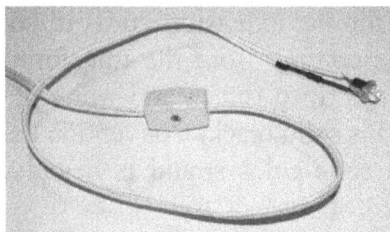

■ **ABOVE.** A 'cord switch' is not a necessity but sure is a convenience. Without it, we must plug in the bulb every time to turn it on and unplug it every time to turn it off. ■

■ **ABOVE.** Don't confuse Rayovac incandescent bulbs with Rayovac LED bulbs. Standing in front of a display of various bulb types and wattages, it's surprisingly easy to go astray. (Especially with your wife standing nearby tapping her foot.) The LED version shown here is what you want and is carried by Walmart. ■

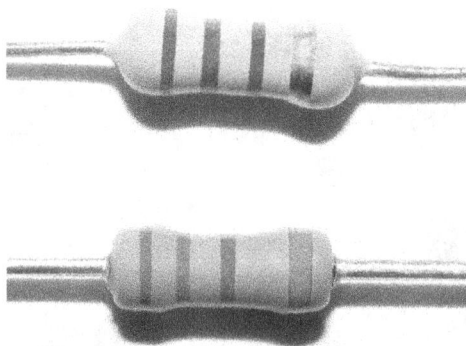

■ **ABOVE.** Resistors are described in Section 6.6. Appendix II explains how to read a resistor's ohm-value from the colored bands. It can be something of a mystery. Although one of these resistors is tan and the other is blue, and one has a gold band and the other a red band, they are both 150-ohm resistors. ■

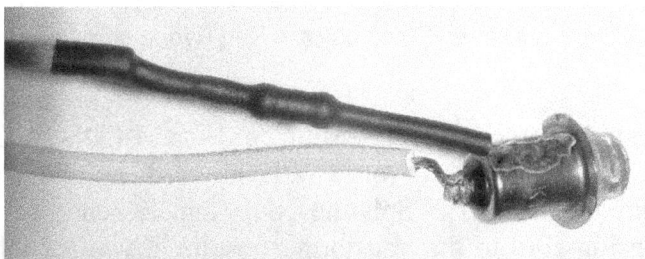

■ **ABOVE.** Here's the business end of the whole affair. The ribbed wire (negative) has been soldered to the center terminal of the LED bulb. One leg of a 150-ohm resistor has been soldered to the side of the LED bulb. (The entire metal side of the bulb case serves as its positive terminal.) The other resistor leg was soldered to the smooth wire (positive) of the extension cord. The resistor was then covered with heat-shrink tubing. You can see the outline of the resistor inside the tubing. It looks like a tiny dumbbell swallowed by a tiny black snake. ■

■ **ABOVE.** Does it work? Did we get a 6-volt flashlight bulb to run off a 12-volt car battery? You betcha, Red Ryder. ■

If desired, you can add extension cords and LED's so as to put a bulb in every room (all powered by the same battery/transformer). Splicing the female end of an extension cord to the transformer results in two (or three) female sockets coming from the transformer. One of these sockets could hold an LED on a short cord while another held a long extension cord. And that long cord would provide another two sockets. One of which could hold a short LED; another could hold a long extension cord. You could continue the chain and have several LED's, wired in parallel, each of which (with cord switches) could be turned off and on independently.

■ **ABOVE.** By my testing, the light output from a single 6-volt LED bulb (including the 150-ohm resistor) was on par with a 71/2-watt nightlight. (Please know it is much more difficult to estimate brightness from a bulb sending out light in all directions than it is with the single, one-directional beam from a flashlight.) If you want more than 71/2-watts, you can eliminate the resistor and boost light output to a 25-watt equivalent. That would reduce theoretical battery life from five years to one year but I suspect most Americans would say, "Who cares? This is EMERGENCY lighting. Let's hope the emergency doesn't last longer than a year. And anyway, I'm not gonna throw the battery away when it runs down. I'm gonna recharge it." ■

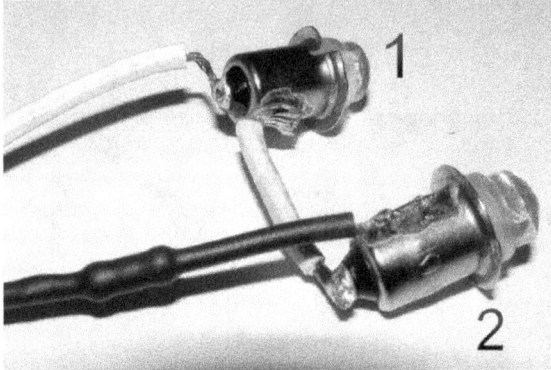

■ **ABOVE.** Here's a way to eliminate the need for a transformer. Instead of one 6-volt bulb plus a transformer we can use two 6-volt bulbs wired in series. That's what's shown here. The ribbed wire from the battery (negative) goes to the center terminal of bulb #1. The smooth wire from the battery (positive) goes to the side of bulb #2. (Here, with the resistor still in place, the end of the smooth wire is covered with black heat-shrink tubing.) A third wire goes from the side of bulb #1 (positive) to the center terminal of bulb #2 (negative). ■

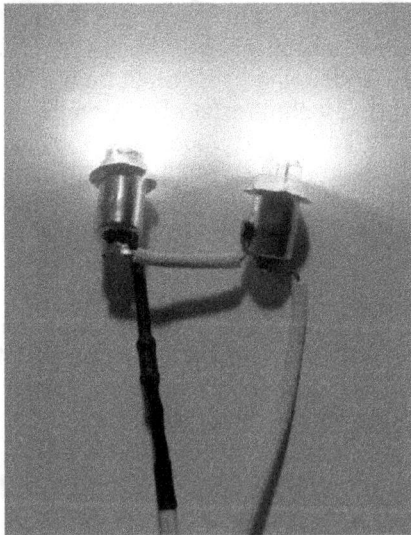

■ **ABOVE:** Here are the two 6-volt LED bulbs wired in series running off a 12-volt battery (no transformer). Total light output for the two bulbs (including a 150-ohm resistor) is 15 watts. ■

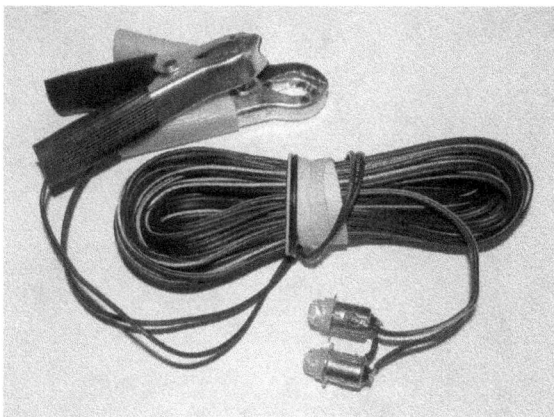

■ **ABOVE.** One more variation, this one appropriate for spending the night in your car. The cord is 25 feet long. One end clips to the battery. (You'll have to open the hood for that.) The other end features two 6-volt LED's wired in series (eliminating the need for a transformer). Light output from this arrangement (with no resistor, please note) is on par with a 50-watt light bulb. In eight hours of running, this configuration will consume about 2% of the car battery's available juice. Unfortunately (as shown here), the cord can flex, allowing the bulbs to touch each other and short themselves out. We'll fix that straightaway. ■

■ **ABOVE.** We're going to hold the bulbs apart by using three nylon zip ties (small ones). One goes around each bulb with its tail pointing towards its neighbor. A third zip tie grabs and holds the tails of the first two. ■

■ **ABOVE.** We've clipped off the dangling tails. The solder residue on the side of one bulb prevents the zip ties from slipping off. And (I tested this carefully) the bulbs get hot but the nylon ties are in no danger of melting. ■

We've probably all left the dome light on in the car overnight and run the battery down. The next morning, turning the key generates silence. Nuttin' honey.

In contrast, LED bulbs are remarkably efficient. The Rayovac LED bulb shown here draws 6 volts and 0.13 amps (according to the package). So two of these bulbs running simultaneously would draw 0.26 amps.

That equates to 1.6 watts (6 volts x 0.26 amps = 1.6 watts). But the two LED bulbs, taken together, generate light equivalent to a 50-watt household bulb. Meaning you get 50 watts of light for 1.6 watts of electricity.

Most car batteries are rated 100 amp-hours or thereabouts. You can draw one amp for 100 hours or 100 amps for one hour. Same difference.

Operating two LED bulbs for eight hours (configured as shown) would leave 98% of the battery's juice untouched, available for starting the car the next morning.

0.26 amps x 8 hours = 2.08 amp-hours consumed

2 amp-hours = 2% of 100 amp-hours (the capacity of a typical car battery)

Ain't science wonderful?

13.0 Liter of Light

A 'liter of light' consists of a discarded soda bottle filled with water and cemented into the ceiling/roof of a shed. Half of the bottle pokes up into the sunshine and half extends down into the room. The water has some bleach in it to kill algae. The bottle absorbs light from outside and discharges it inside. The light produced is on par with a 40-watt light bulb – depending on how cloudy it is that day.

The idea was developed by Alfredo Moser of Brazil and Suryaan Nadeen of New Zealand. In 2011, it was formally launched in the Philippines as part of the My Shelter Foundation.

"**Liter of Light** is a global open source movement with the aim to provide an ecologically sustainable and free-of-cost source of interior light to rooms in simple dwellings with a thin roof." – *Wikipedia.*

Allow me to clarify. My wife is from Manila (Philippines). Metro Manila has a population of 12 million. I have read that squatters (street people) make up 10% of the population. I was once given a personal tour of a squatter's alley. The folks giving me the tour live (today) in a house with chandeliers and marble floors. But they started their married life in that alley. As we roamed the area, children hid behind their mothers and peeked out at me. I felt in no particular danger but I had the distinct impression of treading where white man's foot had never trod before.

The alley was at the back of a warehouse district. Vacant storage rooms and tin-shed extensions were what people called home. Any one room might house several families. The roofs of these sheds were corrugated roofing panels spanning the rafters. No insulation or sheetrock existed between the galvanized roofing and the room below. The rooms were never intended for human habitation. They had no windows. If you entered a shed and closed the door, noon instantly became midnight. The metamorphosis was a shock to the system. *This is the world for which 'liter-of-light' was intended.*

The original 'liter of light' morphed into the idea of using a solar panel topside, out in the sun, hooked up to an LED bulb inside the room (actually inside the water bottle). This is nicely demonstrated in the YouTube video:

http://revolution-green.com/liter-light-night/.

The disadvantage remained that (just like with the original water bottle) when the sun went down the light went out.

So the concept evolved further into the idea of powering the LED with a battery (thus making light available at night), then charging the battery with a solar panel during the day. How to build such a system from scratch (even how to etch the printed circuit board) is shown in the YouTube video:

https://www.youtube.com/watch?v=VhJ36dtsxIA.

For the readers here, please note that you would have the same thing if you added a solar charger to one of the battery arrangements shown in Section 12.0 *Using a 12-volt car battery*. You could charge the battery by day (using the sun) and run the LED at night (using the battery). Solar battery chargers can be found in all price ranges on Amazon and eBay.

Back in the Philippines, today's 'liter of light' is a far cry from its origins (a water bottle gathering sunshine). Today's liter-of-light is a three-step electronic affair – a solar panel that charges a battery that runs an LED.

But the name hasn't changed. The program is still called 'Liter of Light.' If you wear a blue T-shirt bearing the *Liter of Light* logo, I am reliably informed that politically correct native girls will swarm all over you. (Actually, you can skip all the other stuff and just wear the shirt.)

Appendices

I. THE STANDARD

5109LS flashlights (5X variety) as they come from the store produce 25 lumens. To be honest, when I first added a 150-ohm resistor, I was concerned whether or not these lights would produce sufficient illumination to be useful.

They do. Based on a comparison to other lights, I estimate their brightness to be 6 or 7 lumens. Earthshaking? No. Useful? Yes. There are many flashlights on the market that, brand new, produce light in this range.

But now comes the hard part, the question of what to use as a cutoff point, a minimum, a threshold, to say that the 2000-hour light is NOT useful anymore? That's where it gets sticky.

The 5109LS wrapper (5X variety) displays a little clock icon that says "FL 1 Standard 65h" (meaning 65 hours). 'FL 1' stands for ANSI/NEMA FL 1 – Flashlight Basic Performance Standard. In that standard, *run time* is defined as "the continuous time lapsed from the initial light output to when the light is at 10% of the initial output."

So the FL 1 standard uses circular reasoning. A flashlight is measured in terms of itself. If the 5109LS starts out at 25

lumens, when it reaches 2.5 lumens its run time is deemed to have expired. (According to Eveready, that's 65 hours.)

I would argue that we need a fixed standard of comparison, not a moving target. When I'm trying to compare light output and battery life using a 56-ohm resistor versus a 150-ohm resistor versus no resistor at all, a run-time benchmark defined as "10% of wherever you started" is pointless.

So I picked a light that supplies, in my opinion, a minimum threshold of useful light. It's a keychain light, the Maglite Solitaire. It's been around since 1988 and kicks out a blazing 2 lumens. Count 'em. Two.

Although the two-lumen Solitaire will not inspire Tarzan-yells and chest beating, it does produce sufficient light to be useful. You'll be able to find your way to the privy at midnight. It's a practical standard by which to compare various flashlight designs. And it's widely available; Walmart carries it.

With the Solitaire, like every flashlight in the Maglite lineup, the lens cap and reflector can be removed and the light will continue burning – now a 'candle' rather than a flashlight. But that means it can be used as a standard of comparison for battery-powered table lamps in addition to flashlights.

I bought a new Solitaire. The Solitaire's blister-pack contained a Duracell alkaline battery in addition to the flashlight. I swapped out the Duracell for a new Energizer Ultimate Lithium battery. I removed the lithium battery from the Solitaire between tests.

I used a pass/fail test to judge the modified 5109LS. As long as the flashlight being tested was visibly brighter than the brand new Solitaire, I judged the test-light as 'passing.' I would waggle my finger at the test-light and say, "Keep on trucking."

When the light being tested had dimmed to the point of being MERELY EQUAL to the brand new Solitaire, I judged the test-light to have 'failed.' I would then jerk my thumb and yell at the test-light, "You're outta here."

That was my standard. That's where the 2000 hours came from. Please note. The light DID NOT operate at two lumens for 2000 hours. It operated ABOVE two lumens for 2000 hours. When it got DOWN TO two lumens, it 'failed.'

You might well ask, of course, "How did you determine 'visibly brighter'?"

In answer, the simplest test I found was to stand in a dark room with the light being tested in one hand and the Solitaire (the control or standard) in the other and shine the lights in quick succession, one after the other, at an analog wall clock with a sweep second hand, twenty feet away. If you try it, you'll discover there really isn't much question about which one best illuminates the clock face.

The stock Eveready 5109LS (5X variety), equipped with a 'Super Heavy Duty' 6-volt battery, just as it came from the store, was brighter than a new Solitaire for 200 hours. For the next 50 hours it was equal. After that, it produced less light than a brand new Solitaire with a lithium battery.

Luxstar's so-called 360-hour flashlight (see Section 6.5) used a 56-ohm resistor and the Eveready Super Heavy Duty battery that came with the light. For the first 400 hours it was brighter than a new Solitaire. For the next 100 hours it was equal.

Our [original] 2000-hour flashlight (a 5109LS 5X with a 150-ohm resistor and a Rayovac alkaline battery) was, for the first 2000 hours, brighter than a Solitaire/lithium battery combo. For the next 500 hours it was equal.

In all these trials the flashlight being tested faded slowly over time. The stock 5109LS, for example, did not run full speed ahead at 25 lumens for 200 hours and then suddenly collapse to two lumens. Rather, it faded slowly from beginning to end.

II. RESISTOR COLOR-CODING

A word of caution about buying resistors. When you go to Radio Shack and ask for a resistor, the clerk will guide you to a cabinet containing hundreds of neatly labeled packets. He will then abandon you and go wait on the customer who's fondling a $300 cell phone.

Let's say you want a 150-ohm resistor. Be careful that the package says '150' and not '150k.' Lowercase k stands for kilo. Kilo means thousand. And you want a 150-

ohm resistor, not a 150,000-ohm resistor. If you put a 150,000-ohm resistor in your flashlight, not much light will come out.

It's worse online. There you will find resistors with ratings from picoohms (a trillionth of an ohm) to teraohms (a trillion ohms). But you just want plain, old ohms, something without any prefix or suffix.

■ **ABOVE.** The top resistor (tan) is Radio Shack brand. The bottom resistor (blue) is NTE brand. (See Section 6.6 for part numbers.) The color-coded bands reveal they are both rated at 150 ohms. ■

The left-most color band on the resistors pictured above is band **A**. The next band to the right is band **B**. The third band is **C**. And the fourth band, on the far right, is band **D**.

Band **A** represents the first 'significant figure' of the resistor's value. In both of the resistors pictured above, band **A** is brown. And brown, according to the list below, equates to the numeral '1' (one).

Band **B** represents the second significant figure of the resistor's value. In both of the resistors pictured above, band **B** is green. And green equates to the numeral '5' (five).

Band **C** represents a 'decimal multiplier.' In both of the resistors pictured above, band **C** is brown. In its multiplier role, brown equates to the numeral '10' (ten).

The resistance value in ohms for both of the resistors pictured above is 150. Derivation: brown and green represent 'one' and 'five,' respectively. *One* and *five*, grouped together as 15 and multiplied by 10 = 150.

Note that the background color (tan in one case and blue in the other) has nothing to do with the resistance value.

But how do you know where to start? That is, how do you know which end is the 'left' end? Answer. In the blue resistor there is a gap between **C** and **D**. To read that resistor's value, the gap is placed on the right-hand side.

With the tan resistor, band **D** is gold. Gold does not appear in the significant-figure color scheme so a gold band must be a **D** band, not an **A** band.

Band **D** represents the plus-or-minus tolerance of the resistor in percent.

The significant-figure band-colors are the same for both **A** and **B**. And they are:
Black = 0
Brown = 1
Red = 2
Orange = 3
Yellow = 4
Green = 5
Blue = 6
Violet =7
Gray = 8
White = 9

The multiplier-band colors for **C** are:
Black = zero (that is, 10^0)
Brown = 10 (that is, 10^1)

Red = 100 (that is, 10^2)
Orange = 1,000 (that is, 10^3)
Yellow = 10,000 (that is, 10^4)
Green = 100,000 (that is, 10^5)
Blue = 1,000,000 (that is, 10^6)
Violet = 10,000,000 (that is, 10^7)
Gray = 100,000,000 (that is, 10^8)
White = 1,000,000,000 (that is, 10^9)

The tolerance-band colors for **D** are:
Gray ± 0.05%
Violet ± 0.1%
Blue ± 0.25%
Green ± 0.5%
Brown ± 1%
Red ± 2%
Yellow or gold ± 5%
Silver ± 10%
No band ± 20%

So now when you spill a box of resistors on the floor you have at least a prayer of straightening out the mess, yes?

III. TOOLS AND TIPS

In the flashlight world, the word 'hack' (widely used on the Internet) means 'modification.' In this manual our flat-metal-band hacks all follow the same script. The metal band is cut. Each cut end is curled into a loop. After inserting a resistor-leg into a loop it is pinched flat with pliers and soldered (or wire-glued). And if we break something along the way it must be fixed.

We need a way to perform each of these steps. Rather than adhering to a rigid list of must-have tools, let's look in our toolbox and appraise what we already have on hand, then fill in the gaps where we lack the means to perform a step.

First, we must cut the flat metal band. Although tin snips (if we have the right size) are the easiest, sometimes it can be done with just a hand-held hacksaw blade (see Section 9.0, Step 2).

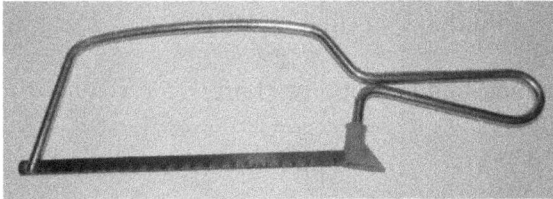

■ **ABOVE.** This is a small hacksaw from the Dollar Store. I have also seen this style saw in a Sears hardware store. And the 'Pasco 4290 Tiny Tim Hacksaw' on Amazon is similar. It will cut both plastic and metal. It works well on the thin metal bands we find inside flashlights because it has 32 teeth per inch. Ordinary hacksaw blades will work but have half as many teeth per inch and chatter on thin material. ■

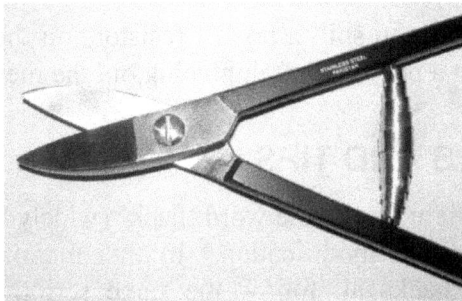

■ **ABOVE.** These snips are Mazbot brand, 7" long, available on eBay for about $15. Size-wise, they're appropriate for tin-can sheet-metal work. They work well for our purposes. 'Gyros 73-01830 Tiny Tinsnip Cutters' on Amazon are similar. ■

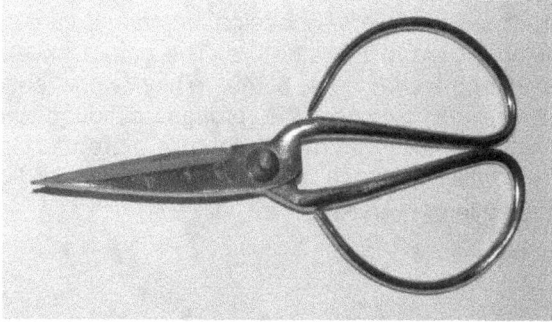

■ **ABOVE.** 'Chinese scissors' work best of all. Mine came from the housewares section of an oriental food market and were $3.49. There was no wrapper so, other than some Chinese characters stamped on the blade, I have no information regarding brand. They are 7" long. At 31/2 ounces they are fairly heavy duty. The needlenose tip requires very little clearance and the scissors are husky enough that just the tip provides a crisp, clean cut on thin metal flashlight bands. Perfect for our purposes. A search on Amazon for 'Chinese scissors' reveals many makes and models. ■

After cutting the metal bands we must form loops in the ends of the bands to accept the wire resistor legs. Needlenose pliers are the obvious choice although special-purpose craft pliers used for bead work, shown below, are a better choice if available.

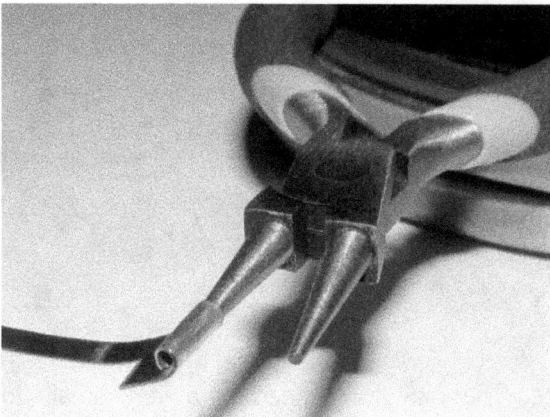

■ **ABOVE.** These pliers are 'Beadalon' brand and came from the bead/jewelry section of a craft store. The ones I have are tiny, only 31/4" long, and cost $3.49. They work better than needlenose pliers because the prongs, although the same diameter, are shorter. That means the pliers are more rigid; the 'nose' doesn't flex as much. On Amazon, search for 'Beadalon Round Nose Pliers, Ergo Style.' ■

■ **ABOVE.** Here we have a Dollar Store hot-glue gun. This can be a useful tool when and if things go wrong. (Specifically, if we break off a plastic rivet-head that holds things together and we need a way to glue the flat metal band – or piece thereof – back in place.) Search Amazon for 'hot glue gun' and you will find them in all price ranges. ■

■ **ABOVE.** You may have need of a very small drill bit (if something goes wrong with your hack and you must cobble it back together). This is a standard set of jobber drills containing fractional-sized, letter-sized, and number-sized drills. 'Jobber drills' are ordinary, garden-variety drills as regards length, material, and grind. The name may be unfamiliar but the drill bits themselves are the most common style or type out there. ∎

The smallest fractional drill is $^1/_{16}$ inches (.0625") in diameter. But the smallest bit in the whole jobber set is a number drill, #60 (.040" in diameter). A #60 hole will accept the leg of a resistor with room to spare. The good news is that you don't have to buy a whole set. Number-sized drills can be purchased individually online (e.g. Amazon) or at brick-and-mortar hardware stores.

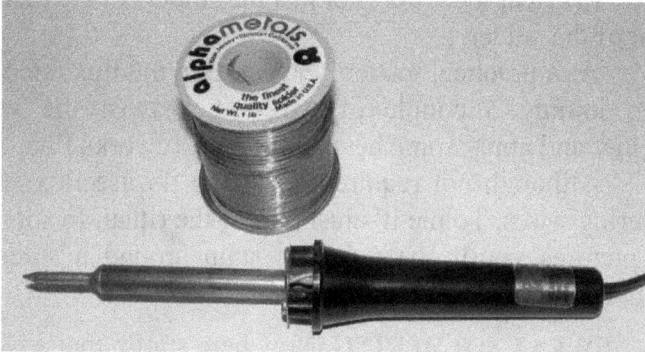

∎ **ABOVE.** Here we have an inexpensive soldering iron. (It may have come from the Dollar Store; I don't remember. A search for 'soldering iron' on Amazon will reveal many brands.) In any event, a cheapie is all we need for the task at hand. Although black wire-glue (see Section 6.6, above) will work on these flat metal-band hacks, to be honest I have more confidence in metallic tin-lead solder. ∎

■ **ABOVE LEFT:** Here we see a metal-band 'loop' with a resistor leg inserted. It has been pinched flat with pliers. ABOVE RIGHT: The same loop after soldering. ■

SOLDERING. I learned to solder in the old days (before plastic). Back when soldering sheet metal was a common fabrication technique for all sorts of household items. And the rules for soldering were these:

(1) Clean the work physically (sandpaper, steel wool).

(2) Clean the work chemically (with flux; sal ammoniac was generic; Rubyfluid was a common brand name).

(3) Heat the work (not just the solder) to the melting point of the solder.

As a practical matter, you can skip the flux (step #2) when joining a couple of wires. Just twist the wires together and apply some heat and solder. It works fine.

Although not required, I usually do use flux when soldering wires. To me it's just part of the ritual. In some of my pictures you'll see a brown stain around a soldered joint. The stain is the flux residue.

SWEAT SOLDERING. Now here's a tip that's worth the price of admission. In 8th grade shop circa 1954 we called it 'sweat soldering' although I'm not sure that was ever the correct term.

Let's say you want to fasten the end of a wire to a metal tab and the tab is located deep inside the flashlight. Simultaneously holding the work together (the 'work' being in two pieces, the wire and the tab) plus getting a soldering iron in there plus getting some solder in there can be nearly impossible without having three hands.

So here's what you do. Lay the wire on the workbench, hold the tip of the soldering iron on the end of the wire, and melt some solder onto the wire. This called 'tinning' the wire.

Next, do the same thing with the metal tab down inside the light. Hold the tip of the soldering iron on the tab and melt some solder onto the tab (that is, 'tin' the tab). A dab of flux won't hurt anything.

Now you have the wire with some solder on it and the tab with some solder on it. Next, using two hands only (you no longer need three), hold the wire on the tab and touch the assembly with the soldering iron. As soon as the solder starts to melt, STOP!

It's done. It's soup. Quit cookin'. Just hold the wire still a moment until the liquid solder cools and solidifies.

SOLDER. Now let's talk about solder, the material itself. You can think of solder as a superglue that will bond metals together; a superglue that adheres to metal and is, itself, a metal.

This superglue (solder) is applied as a liquid. That means it must be melted. That means it must be heated. That's what the soldering iron does. It heats and melts our metal superglue. A soldering iron is a superglue applicator.

Traditional solder was (and is) a tin-lead alloy. When you buy solder, tin-lead solder is the most common and will be the easiest to find. But lead is not good for people and in 2005 the European Union banned tin-lead solder. As a result, today, lead-free solder is also available.

Solder is commonly sold in wire form. The 'wire' can be either solid or hollow (like a tiny soda straw). If hollow, the center contains flux. 'Acid core' solder is used for plumbing. 'Rosin core' solder is less corrosive and is used in electronics.

Don't get too hung up on the acid-core/rosin-core thing. Last year I had some plumbing work done in the basement. The plumber showed me a badly corroded copper fitting he had just removed. Without a doubt the corrosion was caused by acid-core solder having been used in the original installation. In 1963. Fifty years back.

Will the flashlight you're hacking still be around in 50 years?

Personally, if I needed some solder I would most likely go to the workshop and use whatever I found. But if you're unsure (or starting from scratch with no supplies on hand), go to an electronics store such as Radio Shack. They will be glad to help. For sure you will learn something. Even your wallet will be enlightened. Think of it as part of the education process.

Bonus section from Gaye Levy

12 MONTHS OF PREPPING, ONE MONTH AT A TIME

Introduction

Getting prepared, and becoming a Prepper, has got to be one of the more important challenges for families living in the 21st century. The reasons are clear.

We live in an uncertain world with a shaky global economy, extremes in weather, nasty superbugs, risk of an EMP, and threats of cyber-attacks as well as terrorist attacks by militant political regimes. Add to that disappearance of the middle class, Wall Street corruption, and an ever increasing dependence on petroleum products, and indeed, there is cause for worry.

For these reasons, a sizable segment of the population has turned to prepping and family preparedness as a solution to the inherent dependence we have on supermarkets, shopping malls, organized medicine, and government. It is not that these entities are going away, not at all or at least not right now. It is simply that we prefer to be self-reliant and independent of third party interference with our lives.

Preppers, and those that embrace the prepper lifestyle, embrace what is commonly called the "Survival Mindset".

What is the Survival Mindset?

The survival mindset is a frame of mind whereby daily life is focused on the pursuit of independence and self-reliance. This focus is done in a non-obtrusive way to the detriment of no one and the betterment of everyone. It is a lifestyle and a commitment to preparedness and to courage, to optimism and to family values.

Ultimately, it is the will to live and to survive with the knowledge that you have done the very best you can to protect yourself and your family from danger and the woes that come from living in complicated and uncertain times.

What I have just described is also the Backdoor Survival mindset [link below].

http://www.backdoorsurvival.com/

And while I would like to think that it is the very best description out there, I am not arrogant enough to think that what works for me will work for everyone. But, whether you are an experienced prepper or a newbie that is just beginning to get your toes wet, you need to think about your own personal *Survival Mindset* and move to a survival place that meets your own needs.

Getting Started as a Prepper

The roadblocks to getting started on the journey toward preparedness are many.

Time, money and the lack of moral support from **reluctant family members** all play a role in putting off or <u>procrastinating</u> [link below] when it comes to your prepping efforts.

http://www.backdoorsurvival.com/learning-to-overcome-prepper-procrastination/

And then there is fear; not only the fear that **something may happen and** you will not be ready but also the fear of the *something* itself.

Let us put those fears and concerns aside for now and instead, focus on moving forward. Let me help you break down the overwhelming task of emergency and disaster preparedness ("prepping") by providing you with a month by month roadmap of things to do, tasks to complete, and items to purchase.

The goal is to have a manageable number of things to do in a finite amount of time. At the same time, you will be able to do so with a limited cash outlay. And instead of looking at a task list 10 pages long, you will have a short list that is eminently doable in 30 days or less.

Does this sound like a good plan? And are you ready to start?

MONTH ONE SUPPLIES & GEAR:

- Water-3 gallons per person and per pet
- Hand-operated can opener and bottle opener
- Canned meat, stew, or pasta meals – 5 per person
- 2 flashlights with batteries

Let's talk about water first.

Have you ever woken up in the middle of the night with an unquenchable thirst? That thirst is a signal that your body is dehydrated and is lacking a sufficient quantity of fluids to function.

When this occurs, the blood in your body is compromised. More succinctly, it gets completely whacked out. And the result? In addition to increased thirst, dry mouth & throat and chapped lips, all of which are annoying, there is a risk of lethargy, dizziness, decreased urine output, constipation, migraine headaches, wild fluctuations in blood pressure, rapid heartbeat and ultimately, lack of consciousness. Much more, at this point, than a mere annoyance, this can, in fact, be life threatening.

So how bad really is dehydration? Back in 2001 I ended up being carted to the hospital by the local EMTs as a resulted of dehydration caused by food poisoning. My husband thought he was losing me; and was not feeling so great myself. it was not a pleasant experience.

So yes, think about water storage now and make it your number one priority.

There are lots of ways to store water. You can purchase a 55-gallon barrel, you can stock up on bottled water, or, if money is tight and you are willing to do a little work, you can clean and fill some empty soda and juice bottles with water from your tap and store them someplace cool and protected for up to six months. I have written an article on do-it-yourself water storage which you can go back to if you need some guidance with your water storage: Survival Basics: Water [link below].

http://www.backdoorsurvival.com/survival-basics-water-and-water-storage/

The next items on the list are related: canned goods and a manual can opener. The goal here is to put away some food items that you enjoy, that require minimal cooking, are tasty and – here is the rub – are calorie dense. This is not the time to worry about the very best in low fat, diet-friendly foods. What you are looking at are foods that are going to feed your body with energy.

Have you ever analyzed the contents of MREs? (If you are not familiar with that term, MRE stands for "Meal, Ready-to-Eat" such as the precooked and prepackaged meals used by military personnel in combat.) Many such meals seem tiny in quantity by today's standards and yet the total calorie count, per meal, is up to 1,200 calories or more.

The moral of this lesson is that in a crisis or emergency situation, your body needs fuel and fuel means calories. As you are planning your canned food storage items, think calories and lots of them.

One of the easiest ways for a beginner to tackle their initial food storage needs is to open up their cupboard or pantry and raid the contents. And for the more experienced prepper? You are still going to want to take a peek in your cupboards and take a look at the foods you are currently eating and hopefully enjoying. Have you included these with your existing supplies? What better time than now than to go take a look. Pick and choose some new items and add them to what you already have.

Here are some of the canned and prepared food items that I personally have stored away in my survival pantry:

- *Canned chicken*
- *Canned beef*
- *Canned Soups*
- *Canned beans*
- *Canned chili*
- *Mac and Cheese*
- *Peanut Butter*
- *Pilot Crackers in a tin*

For a more thorough list of ideas of food items to store for an emergency, see **20 Items to Kick Start Your Food Storage Plan** [link below]. Keep in mind, however, that this is only month one of the 12 Months of Prepping, and you do not need to stock your entire food pantry at once.

http://www.backdoorsurvival.com/20-items-to-kick-start-your-food-storage-plan/

In addition to food, we have flashlights and batteries on our list of Month One supplies and gear.

This is one area where you are going to want to do a bit better than your 99 cent flashlight from the Dollar Store. Not that I don't love those little LEDs that cost just a dollar each, but in a power outage, you are going to need something a bit more powerful. I happen to **like the Eveready lantern-style flashlights that can be modified so that they last a full 2000 hours** [the link below takes you to a 2013 interview of myself by Gaye Levy, done shortly after publication of the original 2000-hour flashlight book; please know that *this* book – the one you are reading right now – is a new edition and supersedes *that* book].

I also own a number of heavy duty tactical-style flashlights which are dependable and heavy enough to be used as weapons. If you have a few extra dollars, then by all means get a few of **these $4 Mini Crees** [link below] **from** Amazon and stash them around the house, your vehicles, and your handbags and backpacks. You can never have too many flashlights.

> *http://www.amazon.com/gp/product/B006E0QAFY/ref =as_li_ss_tl?ie=UTF8&camp=1789&creative=390957&cr eativeASIN=B006E0QAFY&linkCode=as2&tag=continmot i-20*

And then there are batteries; you are going to want to have lots of batteries. It is all well and good that you are a good steward of our planet and use rechargeable batteries but trust me, in a power out, grid down situation, you will be thankful that you have a healthy supply of standard alkaline batteries as well.

MONTH ONE TASKS:

- *Inventory the disaster supplies you already have on hand, including your camping gear*
- *If you fill your own water containers, mark them with the date they were filled*
- *Date cans of food and food containers if you have not already done so*

The first task in Month One is to inventory your existing supplies, especially any outdoor or camping gear that you may already own. What I did when I first got started prepping is walk around the house, yard and garage, taking note of items I had on hand that could be used if the power were out, if a natural disaster or storm shut down the roadways, or if there was some other crisis.

Here is a list of some of the things you can look for as you undertake a walk-around inventory. This is not a comprehensive list, just some ideas to get you started.

- *First aid supplies*
- *Warm blankets*
- *Outdoor cooking facilities*
- *Cooking fuel*
- *Knives, hatchets and saws (for cutting away brush)*
- *Self-powered radio gear*
- *Sleeping bags & tents*
- *Lanterns*
- *Firearms and self-defense items*

Remember, at this point we are merely taking an inventory so that you can assess any gaps in your gear and begin thinking about the purchases you will need to make in future months. You can also use this time to note the condition of the gear you have on hand and make repairs if any are needed.

Note: Next month we will talk about assessing specific risks so you can better plan for mitigating the consequences of those risks. For now, however, the important thing is to simply take stock of what you already own.

The final task for Month One is to get out those Sharpies or other permanent markers and note the date you filled your water containers and the date you purchased the food you set aside for emergency use. Many will argue that you should mark everything with the expiration date but to my thinking, you need a PhD in code breaking to understand those expiration dates that appear on cans and packaged food.

I feel you are much better served by focusing on an effective rotation system, First In First Out (FIFO), using the approximate purchase date as a rough guideline. Couple that with rotating food and water twice a year when you change the clocks for daylight savings time and you should be all set.

The Final Word

The very first month in implementing a preparedness plan does not have to be difficult, nor does it have to be time consuming or unnecessarily expensive. Please, whatever you do, do not get frustrated. There is a lot of support in the online community, including the kind folks that visit my website [link below] at. Ask a question and surely someone will reach out to help with an answer; if not there then on Facebook [link below] or one of the other social media platforms.

> http://www.backdoorsurvival.com
>
> https://www.facebook.com/thesurvivalwoman

And what if you are a more experienced prepper?

What better time than now to go back and review your progress and perhaps share your experience with an unenlightened family members or favorite friends. Send your loved ones a copy of this article and help them formulate their own survival mindset and preparedness plan.

Be patient and gentle with them if they don't at first understand. In the long run, they will thank you.

--

To continue learning about preparedness, visit the entire **12 Months of Prepping** *series on Gaye Levy's Backdoor Survival website at http://www.backdoorsurvival.com/12-months-of-prepping-year-one/.*

www.ingramcontent.com/pod-product-compliance
Lightning Source LLC
Chambersburg PA
CBHW050534280326
41933CB00011B/1577